HAROLD PINTER

A Study of Cultural Memory

VANDANA GARG

ATLANTIC
PUBLISHERS & DISTRIBUTORS (P) LTD

ATLANTIC
PUBLISHERS & DISTRIBUTORS (P) LTD
7/22, Ansari Road, Darya Ganj, New Delhi
Tel.: +91-11-4077 5252, 2327 3880
E-mail: orders@atlanticbooks.com
Web: www.atlanticbooks.com

Published by Atlantic Publishers & Distributors (P) Ltd 2024

Printed & bound in India by Atlantic Print Services

To my artistic parents,
& my loving husband advocate Virat Garg
who gave me the vision to see grace.

Foreword

It is a matter of great pride and honour for me to introduce the readers to Vandana Garg's scholarly book, *Harold Pinter: A Study of Cultural Memory.* One of the most influential thinkers of his generation, Harold Pinter was not only a renowned British playwright but also an accomplished actor and director. In a successful career spanning over half a century, he wrote as many as twenty-nine plays and acted in a wide range of adaptations of his plays for both television and cinema. *The Room* (1957), *The Birthday Party* (1959), *The Homecoming* (1965), *The Old Times* (1971), *No Man's Land* (1975), *Betrayal* (1978), *A Kind of Alaska* (1983), *Mountain Language* (1988), *Moonlight* (1993) and *Ashes to Ashes* (1996) are some of his well-known plays.

Though Pinter started off in the 'tradition of the absurd', he slowly moved away from it, gravitating towards the 'memory plays'. The existential angst and the unerring sense of menace that often characterised his 'absurdist' plays, however, didn't quite leave him, ever. It continued to manifest itself even in his self-consciously political plays. Often angst, menace, absurdity and linguistic minimalism blended freely with scarred memories, overt hints of political activism and enduring search for identity and truth to create the mosaic of Pinter's oeuvre. With each new play, Pinter's understanding of the complex human experience gained a new cutting edge, deepened and intensified, which he, then, sought to mirror in his multi-layered dramatic representations.

From the searing dialogues of *The Birthday Party* to the enigmatic silences of *The Homecoming*; from the fluidity of memory in *Betrayal* to the inscriptions of trauma and memory in *Ashes to Ashes,* Pinter's works foreground the idea of 'cultural memory' in its myriad forms. The idea of cultural memory was born in the aftermath of the Holocaust, which had resulted in unimaginable suffering and persecution of the Jews in the Nazi Germany, during the World War II. It is in the seemingly mundane and innocuous exchanges of Pinter's characters that we often find resonance of much deeper socio-political questions of his times. Pinter explores the undercurrents of cultural memory through a sustained examination of how identity, memory and politics operate within a hegemonic social structure.

For someone born into a Jewish family, it was but natural for Pinter to acquire a sense of his own past and also that of his ethnic community. The otherness of being a Jew left an indelible imprint on his consciousness, and later found multiple and varied articulations in almost all of his writings; plays, poems, essays, sketches and screen plays, included. His focus on cultural memory was merely an extension of his obsession with his own past and that of his immediate family. In her book, Vandana Garg has succeeded in unravelling the intricate patterns of how individual memories criss-cross and intersect with the multiple layers of cultural memory in the plays of Pinter. Proceeding on the assumption that 'memories' are intertwined with history, politics and culture, Vandana has managed to unearth the artist in Pinter, who knows how to transform the painful, scarred memories of Jewish Holocaust into enduring cultural artefacts.

In exploring the profound impact of cultural memory on Harold Pinter, this book delves into the nuanced interplay between the complexities of 'remembering' and 'forgetting'. It looks into the incisive question of how Pinter's dramatic narratives shape and reflect the broader cultural landscape, bristling with memory, power, human suffering and endurance. Emphasizing the role of both silence and language, this study underscores how the dialectics of the two shapes the individual memories as well as the collective narratives of the communities/societies. While skilfully negotiating the shifting frames of temporality and spatiality in his representations of cultural memory, Vandana's book convinces us that Pinter ultimately does transcend all frames, and attains universalism.

Often while discussing the aesthetics of Pinter's plays, we tend to ignore his role as a political activist and a champion of human freedoms. Pinter, the playwright and Pinter, the activist, can hardly be separated. During the post-Cold War period, Harold Pinter had begun to raise his voice, rather consistently, against the war and its consequent abuses of human rights. He was aware of the fact that the abuse of power and political manipulation only results in the gradual and inevitable erosion of human agency. Pinter's commitment to truth-telling, often in the face of oppressive regimes, positions him not only as a playwright and an activist, but also as a guardian of the ethics of cultural memory.

In 2005, Harold Pinter was awarded the prestigious Nobel Prize for Literature. On this occasion, while delivering his acceptance speech, he stated categorically: "When we look into a mirror we think the image that confronts us is accurate. But move a millimetre and the image changes. We are actually looking at a never-ending range of reflections. But sometimes a writer has to smash the mirror—for it is on the other side of that mirror that the truth stares at us." His words, whether spoken on stage or in international fora, stand a living testimony to an artist's unwavering commitment to truth and his self-chosen act of social responsibility. Pinter's enduring relevance lies in his ability to transcend the confines of theatre, and offer time-tested reflections on power and truth, while traversing the ever-shifting sands of memory, both personal and collective.

The escalating conflict between Israel and Palestine has, in the recent times, put the spotlight back on the perennial questions of 'historical amnesia' and 'evasion of truth' that Pinter so zealously and relentlessly struggled with, all his life. If read against this backdrop, Vandana Garg's book on Harold Pinter acquires a new context, even signification, not only for the students of literature, history and culture, but for the lay readers, as well.

Prof. Rana Nayar
Former Director
Department of English & Cultural Studies
Panjab University
Chandigarh

Acknowledgement

My deepest appreciation goes to Prof. Dr. Rana Nayar, for his unfathomable levels of integrity and knowledge that worked like a lighthouse in the darkest hours of multiple failures & fears throughout this journey of writing.

I sincerely, thank my friend Dr. Ashima Bhardwaj for her kind assistance in editing part.

And finally, my deepest gratitude goes to all who are constantly sending their love & blessings.

Vandana Garg

Preface

Well, there was no problem.
All the democracies
(all the democracies)
were behind us.
So we have to kill some people.
So what?
Lefties get killed.
This is what we used to say
Back in the old days:

—Harold Pinter

This book is based upon the modern critical theory and its various aspects present in Cultural studies and Historiography. An attempt has been made to configure the omnipresent nature of memory in Pinter's Absurd drama, which is full of perverted love stories, arbitrariness and power abuse. Pinter reveals through the family settings in his plays that how one can choose particular memories of the past to built a secure future.

Drama as genre, in itself is an act of remembrance and memorization process, Pinter has achieved the heights of Memory process in his Memory plays. Who, when, how and why someone is narrating one's tale of the past can become a political tool for

State apparatuses or if someone choose to remains 'Apolitical and become an Artistic genius like Harold Pinter.

Memory is the core of human existence; it forms and reforms identities, it enables humans to understand the world that they live in, and it serves as the reservoir of creativity too. Plato believed that within individual memories there were always residual traces of collective memories that hail from past lives too. In this way man was thought to be a combination of his/her present existence, as well as though memory, part of a large collective existence. Man, through the medium of memory grows, learns, interacts and finally acquires an identity. Identities are neither God given nor inborn, so any successful attack on identity will lead into crisis, like trauma, depression, neurotic quest for something to gain power or may sprout into a great work of art, as one can observe most formative aspect of Pinter's own experiences of evacuation during WWI & WWII.

Memory as a faculty is known for the coherence of human identity and history. But there is another side of memory as a site or location of cultural-social disquiet. The never ending disputes of politics, religion and culture from regional to international levels are deeply rooted in human psyche. Past or past experiences cannot be evaporated – its doggedness is the effect of Memory.

Vandana Garg

Contents

1
Introduction

Cultural memories are the memories of a particular event that took shape in a particular time and space. In the case of the Jewish Holocaust, the memories became transcendental and, with time, kept acquiring new values and hues. For the marginalised people, cultural memories of the Holocaust have acted as resisting forces in their daily routine lives. They have touched an emotional chord of their selfhood. Underneath one communal and religious banner, the Jews felt a sense of togetherness in their suffering. For them, cultural memories became a shared domain of commonly experienced past. They projected their cultural design of civil disposition for future generations. They carried forward the memory lanes in their communication through oral traditions, narrations and daily gossip. On the other hand, the texts, scriptures, monuments, rituals and sentimental objects triggered an echolalia in the present time and space. The nation-state built memory reservoirs in the forms of memorials, landmarks, archives and documented particular events in history. However, when people feel that history is only one version of their past, designed by the State to forget rather than to remember, they become more nostalgic or passionate about what had actually happened in the past to their people or to them. Through cultural designs, people can recall the distant past and utilise it in the present time for more firmness and to reassure their identity.

Cultural memory preserves the spirit of particular people. Man has the unique ability to recall a distant past or immediate past, relive it, experience it again and interpret it in the present time when required. As a cultural product, man acknowledges it in his culture and carries forward the very act of memorisation/ socialisation. In this way, cultural continuity remains for centuries, and the whole lived past reaches the future. Cultural memory is not about authenticating past experiences, nor is it necessary for fostering cultural continuity. Instead, its function is to provide meaningful statements about the past within a given cultural context of the present. Remembrance and recollection are powerful tools to embark on a future. Remembering has been a key to survival for Jews. Their identity has its germination in oppression and resistance. World Wars I and II and the Holocaust left an ugly trail of memories. Cultural memory became a narrative in itself which protected, authenticated and enabled the people to relocate their identity. Cultural memory constitutes a counter-hegemonic discourse, which tends to interrogate and subvert the assumption of cultural dominance and hegemony operating within a culture. Though cultural memory is an individualistic articulation, it still has the potential to represent communal and collective consciousness. It essentially suggests a situation where the difference between the individual memory and the collective memory ceases to exist, as the individual is seen as a carrier of collective memories.

After World War II, the horrors of Nazism and the unsaid sufferings of the Jews in Germany, the concept of cultural memory emerged. The personal identity of the entire Jewish race depends upon the continuity and unity of experience of their common suffering through time. The traumatic collective memory of the Jews resulted from the horrors of World Wars I and II. The Jews who had suffered during the Holocaust could not erase the traumatic memories. One can correlate it with Eric Kluitenberg's viewpoint quoted in his essay *Politics of Cultural Memory* (Kluitenberg 1):

> We've been talking all day about identity issues now, and their value. Our recent experiences, however, have taught us that nothing sets people more apart than identity.

Critiquing the idea of a civilised culture, the Jews revealed the ugliness underneath the European prosperity. In the very act of remembrance, the Jews relived an entire past of pain and anguish. Through a constant engagement with the Holocaust memories, customs, narratives, literature and historical accounts, the Jews showcased the reality of Western civilisation. The torch of civility upheld by Eurocentric ideologies was snuffed out when the slaughtering of the Jews came into the limelight.

The term 'cultural memory' was introduced by Jan Assmann, who defined it as the outer dimension of human memory (Rodriguez and Fortier 1). The social and cultural framing of remembrance and oblivion can be visualised through the various patterns of cultural memory. Remembrance of particular incidents became a collective experience for Europeans in general and the European Jews in particular. The State constructed collective memory reservoirs in the form of memorials and landmarks in Europe after the wars. In post-war Europe, culture changed from a culture of production to a culture of consumption. The connection between memories and objects was institutionalised and exploited through trade in souvenirs. Even the memorials, museums and artefacts signified a distant time (antiquity) or a distant place (exotica). These souvenirs authenticated one's experiences and became survival signs of events that lived only through narratives. The memory industry invited everyone to be part of the pleasure of loss and nostalgia. Remembrance became a profitable business for the State.

War memorials became the main features in the cultural memory of the twentieth century. These memorials are tributes to victims of wars on personal, family, regional, communal and national levels. Post-war European culture witnessed the decision to perform such acts openly and at large scale by giving tributes, writing memoirs and making films purely personal but in a social framework. The war memories had become a haunting nightmare for the whole world. The cultural memory of wars appeared in day-to-day dialogue with families on one side and the State on the other.

The various disciplines of psychology, anthropology and theology understand that one's present existence is shaped by recollections of the past and anticipations of the future in the narrative form. Without narrative and memory, human life would have no coherence at all. Memory, however, is only one mode of experience. Memory does not exist in isolation from other modalities oriented to the present and the future. It is also significant to note that the way one remembers, what one anticipates and how one perceives is basically a social act. Cultural memory deals with people, and, in turn, the people reside in their cultural memory—the reservoir of their narratives. It provides them with a communal sense of worth, living a purposeful life and explains the unending questions of birth and death. Various aspects of cultural memory and its role in identity and community formation will be studied in the project.

History is constructed partially from the accounts of witnesses and partially from preserved documents. A culture that exhibits no memory means it has no history, and having no history signifies that it never existed. It is thus customary in any culture to memorise. History is a record of memories of those involved in the events. It becomes a mosaic of non-linear, discontinuous, fragmented and non-chronological representation. It provides a sense of identity as it bridges the gulf between ancestral claims and their progeny. The process of identity formation is revised through a notion of history. In post-war Europe, the State aimed at erasing some events and reconstructing particular memories that could eventually generate a history of its own.

The Nazi Party came to power in Germany on January 30, 1930. It soon found a strong foothold and declared the persecution of the over five lakh Jews residing in Germany (Matthaus and Roseman xxviii). In his autobiography, *Mein Kampf* (1925), Hitler voiced his contempt for the Jews. He wanted to wipe the Jews from Germany's political, intellectual, social and cultural life, stating that Germany should be "cleansed of Jews" (116). Nazis saw the Holocaust as the ultimate solution to solve the Jewish question. The etymology of the word 'Holocaust' can be traced back to the Greek word *holokauston*, which stands for complete (*holos*) burnt (*kaustons*) sacrificial offering to a God. The Holocaust was the genocide of the Jews. Before the outbreak of World War II, legislation to remove Jews from civil society was established. Hitler's Nuremberg Laws of 1935 deprived the German Jews of citizenship and all civil rights. Innumerable laws had been passed to exclude Jews from the mainstream society. Nazis wanted to achieve supremacy through the purity of blood and its rootedness in the German earth. Concentration camps were created where the captives did physical labour. The inmates worked despite exhaustion and disease. They were packed into ghettos before being transported hundreds of miles away by train to extermination camps. Those who survived the journey were then killed in the gas chambers.

Pinter depicted that the narrative that germinated from such atrocities rested in the cultural memory. The process of Jewish identity formation is revised through such a notion of history. Michael Foucault suggests that historically influenced processes often pretend as facts and must be deconstructed (Rodriguez and Fortier 11). The remembrance of the victims and victimisers was a way of preserving the past and articulating it for future generations. The memories of lived experiences from one generation to the next became the source of rebuilding an identity. The discussions about the tragedy were exhibited in Pinter's drama through ellipses, echoes, silences and digressions. Literature played an important role in keeping collective memory alive in a society where the writing of history was a subservient tool for the glorification of the State.

In post-war Europe, the State aimed at erasing some events and reconstructing particular memories that could eventually generate their own history. European culture changed from a culture of production to a culture of consumption. The connection between memories and objects was institutionalised and exploited. Even the memorials, museums and artifacts signified either a distant time (antiquity) or a distant place (exotica). These souvenirs authenticated one's experiences and became survival signs of events (Holocaust) that lived only through narratives. The memory industry invited everyone to be part of the pleasure of loss or nostalgia. Remembrance became a profitable business for the State. Pinter revealed that obsession with the past and nostalgia for the lost world was politicised by the State.

The memories of the lived experiences from one generation to the other have been handed down through traditions, rituals, myths and narratives. The most direct way of recollecting the past is storytelling. A story is, in itself, a sequential order of a memory. It is a narrative that explicates the coexistence of past, present and future. The role of cultural memory through myth is the true history of people. Language is also a myth as it articulates the process of human relations with land and community. Myth is an expression of the tendency to make stories of power out of the life we live in our imagination. Myth is "a language construct that contains the power to transform...of course, it reflects belief...but it is at base a vehicle...." Myth, then, is knowledge shaped by transformative intent:

> Myth may be seen as a teleological statement, a shaped system of reference that allows us to order and thus comprehend perception and knowledge. (qtd. in Hinchmann and Hinchmann 334)

Cultural memory, like myth, has a historical basis. Myths are powerful vehicles for transmitting historical and cultural events and carry a huge amount of cultural memory. Holocaust memories worked as a myth for coming generations through literature, films, museums and art forms. People find their most important meaning in it. It has become a story believed to have been composed about an event in the past that continues to have meaning in the present because it is remembered. A myth, being a sacred story, easily connects people to religious aspects, such as life and death, divine forces, creation, human nature, culture and so forth. Religious and psycho-social themes, well knitted in mythic experiences and time, are very difficult to separate from cultural memory because the private and public realms are deeply embedded in a mythic reference. The contents of a myth are represented in such a way that they cannot be subjected to any change.

Jan Vansina, an anthropologist, wrote in *Oral Tradition as History* that cultural memory starts from a fixed point in the past. The past is not represented as it is but in different symbolic forms, like myths, feasts, celebrations and rituals. All these symbolic aspects change with the passage of time and adapt new shapes and connotations. Thus, the hard distinctions between history and myth seem blurred. Through cultural memory, it becomes easy to look back at the past and reclaim it as theirs (Assmann 112). The knowledge about the past (Holocaust) has been institutionalised in the form of narratives, songs, dances, films, masks, rituals and symbols.

The sketches of past memory cannot exist in isolation from the present and the future. They are carried forth by people in their unique traditions. They also carry culturally specific symbols of a particular time and place. Social groups traditionally pass on, from generation to generation, the chosen pool of memories. They also pass on pre-decided events through the act of narration. Narrative and narration emphasise the active, self-shaping quality of human thought. Its power resides in its ability to create, form and reshape identity. It proves to be a mirror for people to gauge their beliefs, fears and behaviour. Through a narrative, a culture organises and integrates its understanding of reality.

The Hebrew word for tradition (*Masoret*) connotes the efforts to pass on communal memories. The tradition involves stories, myths, symbols and experiences. Traditions transport the whole lived experience through various arts and modes from generation to generation. Jan Assmann explained in a lecture at Henn Academy in 2009 how culture, as a unit, is a non-biologically transmitted memory of the human race. It is the basic knowledge to survive and live a purposeful life. It flows traditionally with parental training and makes a cultural evolution possible. The traditions carry the personal and communal experiences of people—their arts, myths, stories and anything that is part of the emotional frame of human beings. People live in narratives. The discourses provide them the temporal spaces to understand and acknowledge each other. As a result, narratives form a community. They provide a history and a common shared event with a group. Narratives authenticate the existence and provide important benchmarks for non-members to understand their group's cultural identity. Memory has always been the store of narratives. Recollections of the past and anticipations of the future shape the present existence of the people.

The tradition of narrating and passing on experiences witnessed a setback in the twentieth century. Man had lost faith in his fellow human beings. His surroundings had turned to bombarded rubble. A termination occurred in the recalling of any golden past or hailing of a better future. In this sense, the human narrative turned into a mechanical repetition of the horrors. The key memory for the Jewish community was told in the story of *Exodus*, which has been the guiding myth for Jewish identity. It was not the Jewish people that died in Auschwitz, but Christianity. The Jewish theological question after Auschwitz was not only "Where was God?" but also "Where was humanity?" (qtd. in Rodriguez and Fortier 5). Catholic theologian Johann Baptist Metz echoes this when he speaks of *memoria passionis*:

> The only universal category of humanity, open to us... I am not thinking of a memory that only serves to affirm us or to secure our identities—rather the opposite: it calls into question our tightly sealed up identities. It is a dangerous memory...it is a remembrance that does not use sufferings to make us aggressive, but reflects on others who suffer. The failure of humanity, specifically Christian humanity, is not only transmitted through shared memory, but it is a symbol of all that threatens Jewish existence. (qtd. in Rodriguez and Fortier 5)

Cultural memory resides in religion or can be preserved in religious forms where people can easily channel their past experiences. Remembering through religion became an element of survival for Jews, whose identity had long been bound up with oppression and resistance. Cultural memory or blood calling out to blood and its truth are essential elements of memory. The connection between past and present is displayed through ceremonial privileges and activities. The human desire for spiritual narratives is grounded in its connection with the unique, personal consciousness of an individual framed and informed by the larger community. The essential role of religion is to answer questions on existence and cosmic relationships. Religion connects one with ancestors, spirits and God. It reinforces humans' ability to give meaning to all experiences, such as death, illness, famine, birth or suffering. Religion heightens our communal experience of life. Religious ideology demonstrates a spiritual element that is grounded in experience. By examining the emotional structures of religious faith, one can understand the powerful memories that resist or protect the minor groups from assimilating into the mainstream.

Religious, class and family affiliations help construct the manner in which a memory will be interpreted as a cultural memory. The act of remembrance has been maintained through the memory culture for ages. Memory culture is the process by which a society confirms cultural continuity through the preservation of the collective knowledge of lived experiences from one generation to another. Aby Warburg, an art historian, coined the term "social memory" and considered images as the carriers of memory in a culture (Assmann 110). A sacred story easily connects people to religious meanings about life and death, divine forces, creation, human nature and culture. As such, the myth/story of Guadalupe is not only a master symbol because it enshrines the major hopes and aspirations of an entire society but also has transformative potential (Rodriguez and Fortier 12). It is the contemporary story of faith for Mexican Americans. By sharing and retelling Gaudalupe's divine experience, they share the memory of a primordial experience. They internalise this image daily as a divine practice in the process of feeding their faith and identity. The story echoes the reformation of human faith, grace, liberty and identity in present times.

Personal memory is the keystone that supports collective and social memory, but personal memory cannot be understood apart from social forces. Concerning social memory, in particular, means the images of the past commonly legitimate a present social order. It is a thumb rule that participants of any social system must have a shared memory. When the memories of a society's past are segregated, its members have nothing to share, neither experience nor assumptions. The effect is clearly seen when communication across generations is hindered by different sets of memories. Across generations, different sets of memories, frequently in the shape of implicit background narratives, will encounter each other; hence, although physically present to one another in a particular setting, the different generations might remain mentally and emotionally isolated, as it were, in the brains and bodies of that generation. It shows the alienation effect that comes out after a mental jolt resulting from the crowd of unreleased memories. They are locked inside people's brains, where Beckett feels that "nobody comes, nobody goes, it's awful" or "It's icy forever," in Pinter's words. A similar backdrop was witnessed in Holocaust memories and its victims.

The people have different narratives about their past traumas and feel estranged from them too. The process reveals that cultural memory had a definitive sense of historical consciousness. Often considered as a reaction against systematic, willful attempts of official, monumental historiography to suppress historical memories, especially of a very brutal, inhuman nature, it takes on the form of dialectics of remembering and forgetting, as has been emphasised by Jen Brokmeier. He suggested that, in this discourse, narrative practices are of central importance because they combine various cultural symbols, integrating them within one symbolic space. According to him, three narrative orders, that is, the linguistic, semiotic and performative or discursive, of any artwork, are examined, or these constitute a mnemonic system, a symbolic space of remembering and forgetting in which the time orders of past and present are continuously recombined (Nayar 8).

Memory is like a language (medium) that helps in identity configuration and, unsurprisingly, turns into a subject of manipulation. Pinter portrays through his characters how the construction of identity refers to the evaluation of the past, which is subjective, incomplete and often slips away. Sometimes, memory carries forward the interest of a particular group, race or nation and becomes a purely political tool rather than just belonging. Pinter addressed some of the most pressing concerns of modern societies in his plays. The influence of memory can never be eliminated from human practice. Pinter's memory plays are an archeology of explicit as well implicit knowledge of the past. As a result, Pinter's plays project an inevitable presence of the Wars and Holocaust. The recollections of the characters in modern conditions indicate the dilemma and ambiguity of a democratic political identity.

In post-war Europe, the State aimed at erasing some events and reconstructing particular memories to eventually generate a history of its own. Power always tries to build a justifiable narrative of the past that legitimises its deeds to its people. A nation can remember what it wants its people to remember through its people. Memory and identity are inseparable. It is the Jewish urge to live inside one's memory and search for identity throughout his works that become a recurrent motif in Pinter's plays and reveals the power structure of any State. It is through different memory trips, echoes and dreams that the politics of memory operate in the works of Harold Pinter. The war memories moulded the national memory, history and the collective memory of the masses in Europe. Europe has become an urn of identities and personal memories (Kluitenberg 2). The memory remnants of the wars and Holocaust become a shared property of the people and the State.

The State indulged in selling cultural memory in the form of souvenirs and monuments. The world around was ignorant about the tragedies of the war. Therefore, Europe took the lead in advertising the Holocaust. The cultural memories were transformed into sellable objects that could be consumed in the international arena. A trade was cultivated through films, books, articles, photographs, souvenirs, letters, memoirs, media and particularly war cinema. War history was sold in the form of biographies and autobiographies of the victims and victimisers alike. Memories were commercialised through the acts of mourning.

In his dramatic universe, Pinter universalised the human condition so that people could see themselves in his character's place on stage and dare to say that it was their story. He undertakes a comprehensive study of the role of cultural memory through his memory plays. Pinter painted a real picture of society in all his memory plays and raised a question: How could such shattered memories produce reliable identities? Being a Jew himself, Harold Pinter shared the agonising feelings of alienation with the entire Jewish race. Echolalia of the past is omnipresent in Pinter's plays as his characters live in a memory-filled world that, in itself, represents the oppressed psyche. They continuously repeat their past and perform the very act of mechanical repetition instead of remembrance in their present.

Pinter had immense belief in the power of memory. His personal memories of evacuation during the Holocaust later became an inseparable part of his memory plays. These plays dealt with the loss of memory and post-Holocaust identity reconstruction. His characters lived at the fringes of an emotional no man's land. Pinter spoke to the people in their idiom through a particular medium of absurd theatre, met them face to face and dared to question the whereabouts of humanity in the Nazi regime. Jews had been thrown out of the mainstream society.

Therefore, being a Jew, Pinter joined his peripheral race and voiced their fears, deformed sense perceptions and anxiety in his works. His efforts can be observed as the effect of a collective unconscious in which a poet, guided by the unexpressed desire of his people, recreates the sufferings by word or by actions on the stage. He seeks an answer for the existence of such a fluid sense of self that has been manipulated by autonomous power figures, such as politicians and dictators. Pinter brings the real historical past to the fore and thus challenges the established notions created by the political set-up of the State apparatus.

Pinter revealed that obsession with the past and nostalgia for the lost world could easily be politicised by the power structures. His plays communicate feelings, emotions and experiences that the playwright sees and then meditates upon the perception of the audience and readers. Pinter wrote:

> I'm very conscious of what's happening in the world. I'm not by any means blind or deaf to the world around me... No. No. politicians just don't understand me. What, if you like, interest me, is the suffering for which they are responsible. (Scott 10)

The book is divided into three segments. The divisions explore obsession with particular past memories, the inheritance of such haunting past in present life and the cultural memory of that past event. The focus would be on scrutinising the commoditisation of memory in the hands of the power. It is the power that can rewrite the past narrative according to the needs of the present and make it sellable for the future as well. In doing so, Pinter is able to critique a culture that prides itself on being civilised. Through snapshots of cultural memory, he exposes the propaganda of civility. He raises the vital question of whether the trauma can be forgiven or rewritten whenever needed.

For a victim, everything comes back, and a reactivation of prior suffering takes place. But for the next generation, who is the direct victim or onlooker of the past, it is very difficult to fess up the burden of the past. Thus, commoditisation becomes more important for future generations to carry forward the past in this manner. Pinter deals not only with the memories of survivors but with their effect on people, especially Jews, whose progeny relive the horrors through cultural memory. The power structures utilise the cultural memory to evoke the frozen moments of the past, give it a direction and circulate it for future political benefits. Through the obsession to recall and relive past episodes, Pinter challenged the normalcy that was being promoted by the power apparatuses. The victims were the real-life embodiments of the brutal past that generated a counter-discourse subverting the ethical masks of civility.

The second chapter, 'Obsession with Memory', explores the characters' obsession with their own traumatic past. The obsession with memory can be considered a craving for lost identity, space and existence. The argument undertaken in the chapter reflects Pinter's conception of Jewish identity, which was injured in war trauma and tortured during the Holocaust. Pinter deals with human isolation and the crucial problem of communication through the characters' attempt to recall the past. In this regard, Anna Reading said that memory was not merely an obsession of the twentieth century. It was something central to human existence. Pinter's plays *Old Times*, *No Man's Land* and *Betrayal* project how past memories can become tools of exploitation by the State to gain a psychic advantage over the masses. The obsession became nostalgia for the past or merely a persistent fear of oblivion. Under these conditions, the "present" kind of dwindles between the past and the future without any legitimate sense of inheritance.

The chapter analyses the obsession with memory and its proportional relationship with the fear of forgetting the past. For Jews, the Nazi brutality was enough to throw their life out of gear. The Jewish narrative was deconstructed in the time and space continuum. In search of identity, a community, a race or a country always comes together. Thereafter, the group fosters various traditions and rituals that strengthen their distinctiveness. The State constructs collective memories in the form of commemorations that bind groups and individuals with conflicting agendas. The political leaders narrate the past for their own benefit. A group's cultural memory, projected in Pinter's drama, then becomes a crucial area of study to understand the equation between the periphery and the centre that has shaped post-war European culture. His characters reside under constant fear of "knock at the door" (Billington 82).

The chapter focuses on the struggle for the reclamation of identity through cultural memory. The past becomes a living reality for the characters and is relived through obsessive behaviours. The characters undergo the condition of neurosis, which is the product of the struggle between the interests of self-preservation and the claims of libido. A mental struggle ensues in which the ego has the tendency to emerge victorious, but only at a great cost in terms of suffering and renunciation. The neurotic personality, residing in a particular time-space continuum, is affected by an existential crisis. Ted Bogacz wrote in his essay *War Neurosis and Cultural Change in England, 1914–1922* that World War I had changed the mental behaviour of both the onlookers and the victims of the war. It also challenged the inherited social and cultural ideas and knowledge, including traditional views about the whole world, including mental illness and its treatment. The English veterans who suffered from war-induced mental illness or shell shock raised the most complex questions about the culture and its host institutions (Bogacz 227). The movement from a normal time zone to extreme brutality transformed the character's state of mind. The obsession with the past gave birth to neurotic tendencies witnessed among sufferers and witnesses.

A palimpsest study of the plays *A Kind of Alaska* and *Moonlight* is undertaken in the third chapter, titled 'Inheritance of Cultural Memory'. Pinter's characters are caught in a dark past—where memory intermittently comes and goes whenever they get stimulated. Pinter has revealed all the stages of human memory, including the crisis of inheritance in his plays. He portrayed modern man's struggle with traumatic war memories. His characters constantly fight with the past that they have inherited. The chapter focuses on the process of inheritance of Jewish cultural memory. Past events have a deep impact on what one does and how one will live in the future.

Lamarck's law of inheritance of acquired characteristics and Heackel's theory of ontogeny suggested that an individual is a summation of the whole history or past that has preceded them (Connerton 72). Jews have inherited a past through oral and written accounts and narratives. The fact is that the terror of trauma exists because painful memories have their own survival time. They have once been very powerful and have left almost an indelible impact on a culture, affecting the normal course of daily life. People obsessed with the past inherit a past and bequeath the same to their progeny. The cultural memories they generate have the potential to hinder other facets of all memory types.

Pinter explores such memories and their ability to create coherent yet fragmented identities. Such dormant war memories are located in the mental and material spaces of society. One can observe a kind of cultural neurosis after the World Wars and the Holocaust in particular. The events have become an inseparable part of cultural memory. Pinter directly approaches the collective remembrance and, at the same time, reveals the underlying political façade behind commemoration.

The fourth chapter, titled 'Cultural Memory and Politics', constitutes a study of *Ashes to Ashes* and *Celebration*. Power always tries to build a justifiable narrative of the past that legitimises its deeds to its people. The war memories moulded the national memory, history and the collective memory of the masses in Europe. The memory remnants of the wars and the Holocaust become a shared property of the people and the State. The political framework, which was damaged by the Nazis, had to be repaired in order to rectify the nation's past. The German government had debased it during the wars. A Holocaust memorial was constructed near the Brandenburg Gate in Berlin. It was a part of the political ideology to consolidate a new identity for the Europeans that could equate Jews with other social groups. Its construction was considered a metaphorical rebirth of the German nation or identity. The newly born European economic culture was bestowed with unique political and moral signification.

The chapter elaborates upon the devices of the State apparatus that was hell-bent on deceiving people of their social memory. The totalitarian states practice a kind of mental enslavement by selectively deleting and celebrating particular memories of groups. The process is called organised forgetting oblivion or collective amnesia. Scholars like Ellie Wiesel and Jay Winter stand for oppositional history based on social memory only. Therefore, people now realise that their struggle against the State apparatus is basically a fight for their own memory (Connerton 15).

Literature played an important role in keeping collective memory alive in society and voiced the silence of the oppressed, whereas the writing of history has become a dedicated tool to glorify the State. Through his plays, Pinter challenges the totalitarian system by exposing reality. Pinter projects the debunking of the real historical past by the State. Whatever the State may construct, every individual narrative continues to haunt Pinter's characters. Through different memory trips, echoes, ellipses and dreams, he shows how the politics of memory operates within a system.

The book is an attempt to understand Pinter's restoration of subjectivity, which is threatened with extinction, especially under multiple hegemonic historical oppressions. In the early phases, Pinter focuses on the absurd manners of the modern man's situation. But in the later phase, Pinter takes a political stance. People have been exploited by power through the official narratives of medical science, law, bureaucracy and political system. Pinter defined how the official narratives are approved by power, of power and for power.

Through his dramatic art, Pinter upholds the narrative of the oppressed (Jews). In order to gauge the cultural index of a nation, its cultural memory needs to be analysed. In it lies the power to challenge national history and bring forth the ultimate truth.

The understanding of the past is always incomplete in a political rendition. The actual social phenomenon, as Pinter displays, could only surface in the space between cultural remembrance and history. The undercurrent of collective memory links multifarious aspects of its obsession, inheritance and ultimate commoditisation. For Harold Pinter, it was only through the work of art that historical reality could possibly be deconstructed.

2
Obsession with Memory

> Did you wash the dead body?
> Did you close both its eyes?
> Did you bury the dead body?
> Did you leave it abandoned?
> Did you kiss the dead body?
>
> —Harold Pinter

War and its aftermath paralysed the process of remembrance and memory formation that lies at the core of identity formation. Memory is often known as a faculty constituting man's consciousness and self-awareness, through which the coherence of identity, culture and history is constructed and sustained. World War II and the Holocaust completely changed the traditional nature of remembrance. The ghost-like shadows of the Great War in Europe haunted the collective/social acts of remembrance. People felt insecure. They became obsessed with their past due to the sudden snapping of the link with their own inheritance. The war images and experiences disrupted the narrative of the people's lives. Such disturbances created a shattered identity in the twentieth century. War scenes were so powerful that they blocked the continuum of life.

The Enlightenment (the Age of Reason) invoked a kind of intellectual thinking innate to religious aspects in Western philosophy. Modernism changed the cultural trends and transformed Western society in the late nineteenth and early twentieth centuries. Modernity was connected with the cultural and intellectual movement of 1436–1789 and extended to the 1970s and beyond. In Europe, Modernism introduced an academic culture by including Secularism, Marxism and Existentialism. Modernity renewed and reshaped religious faith, traditional ways of thinking, architecture and social institutions. It gave birth to a new social, political and economic world. The most important feature of modernism is self-consciousness, which leads to new experimentation in art forms, thought processing, philosophy and social designs. Modernism shaped the industrial societies and the rapid growth of the cities and was then followed by the horrors of the World War. The post-war culture was based only on economic power and individualism.

The story of the World Wars and the Holocaust was interpreted by various institutions and print media, garnering popularity in the public domain. The victims of traumatic war memory were inhabitants of a duality. They were residing in the present but were continuously recalling their horrid past. A mere sound, smell or sensation stimulated a barrage of memories of atrocities committed at the hands of the Nazis (Winter 11). As a result, the recollections of a shared past created a common pool of historical remembrances that evoked involuntarily.

Being a Jew, Pinter shares his traumatic past with the whole Jewish race. The seeds of his plays, characters, situations and language are embedded in the collective memory of the Jews and the multiple recollections of their suffering. In one of the interviews with Barry Davis in 1991, Pinter recalled how his school friends were exiled from their homes, and the worst thing that happened to them was that they were declared "as dead." Pinter said that a man turned to me and asked: 'I suppose you're a filthy Yid yourself.' So I said: 'You know, you really must not say that kind of thing to me or to anybody else. You've got to stop saying it.' He said: 'you want me to say that again? He said it again: you're a filthy Yid.' Then I hit him...the man came up to me and said, 'Are you a Jew? And I said 'yes' and he said:

> Well, I can understand why you hit me, but why did you hit me so hard?' I hadn't expected this to happen when I walked into the bar, but it did happen and my fury with

> him came from some part of my being which I didn't consciously analyze or think about. (qtd. in Batty 97)

The characters in Pinter's plays exhibit neurotic tendencies. Ordinarily, neurosis is an expression of disapproval used for a person who is lazy, scared, indecisive, sensitive, demanding or suspicious. But if one perceives the impact of cultural circumstances on neurosis, one can trace biological and physiological conditions to be the ultimate cause of neurotic tendencies. Neuroses incorporate various aspects of masochism, paranoia, guilt and a desire to dominate and control. All these symptoms could be observed in the anxieties of the modern man. Neurosis could then be said to be a product of a struggle between the interests of self-preservation and the claims of libido that attain a victory at great peril in terms of suffering and abstinence (Horney vii).

A person suffers from neurosis when they are unable to face the hostility of the world. The human tendency is to seek love, concern and care, which is a direct way of reaching out to other social elements. But when a person fails to get help from his surroundings, they suffer from neurosis. The neurotic imbalance is born out of anxiety, hatred, guilt and a sense of inferiority. The cultural factors surrounding a person play a decisive role in leading them to neurosis. Even the social structures that symbolise power offer a feeling of greater security. On the contrary, a situation in which there is an absence of social structure support would invite neurosis. The neurotic would always crave power, something that they lack. Their mania for control would also lead them to curtail the freedom of other people. The attitude of impatience thus generated projects their constant will to bring everything under their control.

In *The Neurotic Personality of Our Time*, Karen Horney has suggested how neuroses are generated not only by incidental individual experiences but also by the specific cultural conditions under which one lives. In fact, the cultural conditions are not only an architect but also colour the individual experiences. The obsession with the past has created neurotic tendencies among sufferers and witnesses too. Neurosis is a state of mind that is full of self-contradictory situations. Confrontation with the real world is difficult for a neurotic personality. It is mental conditioning that forbids them from understanding real-life experiences. At times, people become neurotic deviants and perverts because society does not allow them any privacy in the name of sustaining the values of a culture. European history is full of such accounts whereby suppression of the real self gave birth to neurotic tendencies among the masses, creating anxiety in their culture. They have carried forward this neurotic behaviour for generations, and writers like Pinter have investigated the Holocaust in their plays.

The history of the Holocaust is always based on facts, whereas the memory of trauma is an expression of the lived experiences with deep emotional overtones. In his autobiography, *Mein Kampf* (1925), Hitler declared his contempt for the Jews. He had warned to drive them out of Germany's political, intellectual and cultural life. In 1922, he allegedly told Major Joseph Hell, who was a journalist at that time, that:

> Once I really am in power, my first and foremost task will be the annihilation of the Jews. As soon as I have the power to do so, I will have gallows built in rows—at the Marienplatz in Munich, for example—as many as traffic allows. Then the Jew will be hanged indiscriminately, and they will remain hanging until they stink; they will hang there as long as the principles of hygiene permit. As soon as they have been untied, the next batch will be strung up, and so on down the line, until the last Jew in Munich has been exterminated. Other cities will follow the suit, precisely in this fashion, until all Germany has completely cleansed of Jews. (Hitler 116)

Etymologically, the term "Holocaust" is derived from the Greek word *holokauston*, meaning a complete (*holos*) burnt (*kaustons*) sacrificial offering to a God. The Holocaust was the genocide of the Jews. Nazis called it the final solution to the Jewish problem. Legislation to remove Jews from civil society was enacted years before the outbreak of World War II. Concentration camps were established where the inmates were used as slave labour until they died of exhaustion or disease. They were crammed into ghettos before being transported hundreds of miles by train to extermination camps where, if they survived during the journey, the majority of them were killed in the gas chambers.

The most notorious physician was Dr. Josef Mengele, who worked in Auschwitz. He experimented on them in pressure chambers, tested drugs on them, froze them and attempted to change their eye colour through brutal surgeries and by injecting chemicals in the children's eyes. Vera Alexander, a Jewish survivor of Auschwitz, remembered one set of twins in particular—Guido and Ina, both aged about four. One day, Mengele took them away. When they returned, they had been sewn together, back to back. Their wounds were infected and oozing out pus. They screamed day and night. Their mother, Stella, managed to get some morphine and killed the children in order to end their suffering.

Jews were humiliated, used in hormone experiments and surgeries by the doctors and were killed. Nazis forcibly threw them out of their dwellings. As a result of the atrocities, Jews lost the very sense of a unified human being. Pinter evoked a sense of threat, insecurity and anxiety, presenting a naked human condition of modern times. His characters are so scared that they are literally trembling with fear of being stripped off. It is an imposed nihilism that they find themselves in.

Pinter spoke to the people in their idiom through theatre, met them face to face and dared to question the whereabouts of humanity in the Nazi regime. He becomes the collective voice for his people or community as he has become for Europeans (both victims and onlookers). Jews were persecuted and ostracised from mainstream society. The Jewish narrative lost its trace in the time and space continuum. All human concepts died for them. Therefore, being a Jew, Pinter found himself in the same situations as other Jews, and his suffering deformed his sense perceptions the way it did for millions of others. A work of art is a metaphor that contains a message for the generations. It is true for Pinter as much as it is true for any other writer. This happens under the effect of the collective unconscious in which a poet or a leader projects himself to be guided by the unexpressed desire of his people and creates by word or by deed the way of healing his people (Jung 153).

A hell was designed by the Nazis for the glorification of the State and sacrificial offering to their land and blood. In all acts of remembrance, history and memory were knitted together in the public domain, jointly informing the shift in European culture and wrestling with the understanding of the past. Winter has suggested that it is not just the injuries of the war but also its drama, its earthquake-like character, which has ignited the memory boom of the twentieth century. It was a systematically planned obsession with the past. He is of the view that cognitive psychologists reinforce the notion that:

> The act of recalling the past is a dynamic, shifting process, dependent on the notions of the future as much as on images of the past. The memory is the product of a multitude of impulses, drawn together in the form of collage, or approximation of a past event. (Winter 154)

The obsession with the past has led to neurotic tendencies among victims and victimisers alike. People have lived with this neurotic behaviour for generations and occasionally even tried to investigate it. In Pinter's plays, the memory is like an underground river of recollections that will rupture when triggered by some external stimuli.

The nihilistic post-war environment had created a definite problem. People were uneasy with their own reality and sense of being existent. Multiple contradictions were impinged upon their minds and in their lives too. Everyone was caught in their own situation. The people were trapped in the marshland. Creeping out of it became a repetitive act that was equally futile. They were carrying their own versions of the war, but nobody was sure about what actually had happened to them. In Pinter's plays, the characters recall and passively argue over the past because there is no valid proof of what had happened in their past. They fight over petty things and seem more obsessed as they are unable to adjust to their contemporary situation. Their fake combats or mere verbal ping-pong acts as filler. Their behaviour patterns reveal neurotic tendencies. For instance, in the plays, the characters are engaged in verbal dual to gain an advantage over each other. Their repetitive behaviour patterns, including multiple sexual encounters, useless discussions over petty things (like stealing panties in *Old Times*), unusual mental and physical actions such as crawling on the floor or forgetting names, over-possessiveness in relationships (keeping photograph albums as an authentic proof of real friends) and multiple betrayals and lies about extra-marital affairs depict vagueness. David Novitz believes that:

> The human identities are neither God-given nor inborn but are acquired as man grows, develops and interacts with people around him/her under given cultural conditions. (qtd. in Hinchmann and Hinchmann 151)

So, any possible attack on the self-image would give birth to an imbalance of personality, a kind of trauma, depression and neurosis. For example, shell shock is a condition during war times in which the connection between the memory and identity of an individual is disturbed or blurred.

The German term *Angst de Kreatur* states that all of us are helpless in the face of the forces that are more powerful than ourselves, such as death, illness, old age, catastrophes of nature, political events and accidents. Anthropologists also believe that feelings and attitudes are deeply affected by cultural conditions. Cultural and personal derives are inseparable. The standards of what is normal vary from culture to culture (Horney 94). Normal is generally said to be inclusive of a socially acceptable attitude. However, a neurotic goes beyond the anxiety exhibited by a normal inhabitant of society. They either have to dominate or obey. It is their repressed anger and anguish that spurts forth in the form of depression. "A person's ruthless desire to dominate others or for gaining prestige reflects itself into humiliation of others, especially those of the loved ones" (94).

The neurotic secretly desires that the world around them should transform according to their needs. The striving for power for such change demands the deprivation of others' identities, as it happens in Pinter's plays. Neuroses are the cost that humanity has paid and shall continue to pay for cultural development in the future too. The variations in character formation from individual to individual and culture to culture are due to the varying degrees of suppressions in cultures, as seen in Pinter's characterisation in *Old Times*, *No Man's Land* and *Betrayal*. Actually, the neurotic fear emerged during war times and engulfed the great European culture later in the twentieth century. It became a kind of cultural neurosis after the World Wars, especially after the Holocaust.

World Wars and Holocaust-like traumatic experiences have brought about changes in cognitive memory. Memory is often known as a faculty constituting man's consciousness and self-awareness, through which the coherence of identity, culture and history is constructed and sustained. Richard Terdiman seeks to understand modernity's relationship with memory, in particular, with some of the stresses that have characterised that relationship. In a modern world of rapid change, memory has become extremely complicated and unreliable because there is no validity.

In the modern era, especially after the Great Wars, the memory process is in crisis and it has become difficult to recall and carry forward the haunting past. The very coherent order of time and subjectivity has broken down and become disarticulated. The European society, memory and identity had faced an abyss in time and narrative order. Right from the beginning of the nineteenth century, the past had turned into a foreign province. According to Terdiman, there were two main reasons for this. Firstly, the most powerful perception was that of a massive disruption of traditional forms of memory. Secondly, the institution of memory and history became critical preoccupations in an effort to think through what intellectuals had begun to call 'the modern' (Terdiman 5).

The nineteenth century became a present whose self-conception was framed by a disciplined obsession with the past. It is an important fact that the European generation inherited the obsession with memory. From the 1890s to the 1920s, the obsession with memory was focused on the formation of identities, especially national identities (Winter 23). Although social, cultural, communal, familial and personal identities were preserved in mind as well. Remembering the outbreak of the Great War was a very important factor. The second phase, spanning from the 1960s to the 1970s, endorsed a large part of the remembrance, including the Holocaust and World War II, as suggested by Winter. Here, one can see the reclamation of the past identities (for Jews), particularly in Pinter's plays. Digging the past is not just a pastime game for his (supposed Jews) characters. In fact, they are searching for something substantial like identity or community to stand for and live for.

Harold Pinter has painted a truthful picture of this phenomenon in his memory plays and raised the question of how such "shattered memories" can produce reliable identities (qtd. in Winter 53). His memory plays are bare acts of narration, repeating past events and memorisation. He shows how memories can be used as weapons of personal and political advantage. His plays deal with newly occurred anxieties of modern man, and he reveals how the past memories of the Holocaust affect the characters as well as the audiences. One needs to understand modernity's relationship with the memory processing of his characters, particularly with the anxieties that have characterized their relationship with vanished memories and modernity.

Obsession is basically the nostalgia for the past and a persistent fear of oblivion. Under these conditions, the 'present' kind of dwindles between the past and the future without any legitimate sense of inheritance (Winter 53). The sickness of the lost past had been shifted from communal groups to individuals among family members, as exhibited in Pinter's plays. Thus, the narrative about the same past has appeared with many versions as each character had his own memory of the past, but nobody knew the exact truth and the right to validate it. The demarcation between personal and political was shattered. In recent years, many people have come to look upon memory as a way out of the confusion created by the fragmentation of their identities. The term 'memory' has become a metaphor for ways of casting about in the ruins of earlier identities and finding elements of what has been called "a usable past" (Winter 18).

Being a genius, Pinter has transformed his personal experiences of war into his dramatic art. A common element of Pinter's work is memory and yearning for a secure past as a dream where one feels comfortable. Pinter rejected the possibility of philosophical certainty and negated the satisfactory end in dramatic art. An artist is a "man" in a higher sense, as he shapes the unconscious, psychic life of mankind. Art is a psychic product, without a doubt (Jung 151). The poet's work is an interpretation and illumination of the contents of consciousness, of the unavoidable experience of human life with its external reoccurrence of sorrows and joys. The work of art always takes inspiration from the vast realm of conscious human experiences from the vivid foreground of life.

> Art carries its life from the hinterland of man's mind - that suggests the abyss of time separating us from pre-human ages, or evokes a superhuman world of contrasting light and darkness shaping and reshaping - the eternal spirit's eternal pastime. (Jung 153)

Pinter perceived that if it wasn't the religious consent, it surely was the cultural one, particularly with respect to the Holocaust. He believed that poetry and art that had emerged from the Holocaust were very strong and left a very strong impression. Pinter resisted any kind of oppression. He rejected the Jewish religion, argued with his father over the current Israeli policy, and, at the same time, questioned how he could be anything else—especially after the collective experience of Jewish suffering (Billington 17). Pinter may have inherited the Jewish sufferings on the one hand and an artist's liking or disliking of the Jewish identity on the other. In any conventional play, the dramatist conveys whatever he wants to pass on to the audience through words and gestures. But in Pinter's plays, one can look in between, above, under or beyond words or beyond the present, either into the past or the future. The audiences have to work over the creative slant in characterisation, linguistic twists and journey back in the corridors of Jewish history, peeping into the future through cultural memory.

Pinter freed drama from its old-fashioned shackles and induced new meanings into it. The dialogues, situations and characters speak for themselves throughout the play. He never imposed dramatic language, which should be full of honesty, sincerity or innocence, to deteriorate the art of theatre. His diction is essentially human and, of course, made up of lies, exactly like the contemporary social-political system. Pinter himself believed in this fleeting nature of memories and said:

> There can be no hard distinctions between what is real and what is unreal, not between what is true and what is false. A thing is not necessarily either true or false; it can be both true and false. (qtd. in Batty 1)

Memory is transcendental in nature and surfaces in Pinter's work, particularly in the recollections that characters cannot avoid. However, the recollections allow them to drift back into a time when everything was certain and familiar. Their memories tell them who they are and who they were. Pinter seems to say that memories shape and reshape the present according to the needs of the time and situation of each character. And at the same time, memories shift the tones and, at times, slip from their grasp. One may find truth and comfort in one's recollections as Pinter's characters often do in plays, but these reconstructions of the past can never be trusted entirely. In a world where memory is unfixed and provisional, the past can be manipulated to gain an advantage. This aspect projects one of the major neurotic obsessions of Pinter's characters in the play *Old Times* (*OT*). Pinter shows how the characters create the past as a weapon of psychological domination. He himself acknowledged in a *New York Times* interview with Mel Gussow in 1971:

> I think I'm more conscious of a kind of ever-present quality in life… I certainly feel more and more that past is not past, that it never was past. It is present. That fact is that in our emotional lives, the present is constantly shaped and informed the past. Everything is obscure. (qtd. in Billington 211)

Old Times is a comedy of manners that is based on the love affairs of sophisticated young high-ups, who largely rely on their witty expressions in the comic style of popular entertainment. But comic expressions are ironic in a manner to create ambiguity. The play takes place in a London farmhouse of Deeley and his wife Kate in a 1970s social milieu. Deeley and Kate are awaiting the arrival of Anna, who is coming from Sicily after twenty years. The husband and the wife are quite insecure about her arrival as they already know that Anna's arrival could be a threat to their secure world. The play begins with the dialogue between Kate and Deeley. They were smoking cigarettes and discussing Kate's old friend Anna. It starts under dim light when three figures are discerned:

> Deeley: *slumped in armchair, still.*
>
> Kate: *curled on sofa, still.*
>
> Anna: *standing at the window, looking out.*
>
> *Silence.*
>
> *Lights up on* Deeley *and* Kate, *smoking cigarettes.*
>
> *Anna's figure remains still in dim light at the window.* (Pinter, *Old Times* 7)

It appears as though the characters have been plucked out of time. The opening conversation between Deeley and his wife Kate about old friend Anna, whose arrival is clearly expected at any moment, creates suspense about future happenings. Kate says she is her (Anna's) only friend, but Anna has many other friends. Deeley says he had never met Anna and is surprised to know that Kate and Anna were roommates twenty years ago. Kate says that Anna occasionally stole her underwear.

In the next scene, Anna reaches their place, and they share good memories of the past. Deeley talks about his past as a sailor and tells Anna that he had met Kate at a movie and had asked her out for a cup of coffee. After the conversation, the characters became silent, and Anna went to bed. Kate, too, went to sleep, and a man was heard sobbing in the darkness and walking around Kate's bed. After some time, he lay in Kate's lap and then went out. Kate neither confirms nor denies these tales and eventually goes for a bath. While Kate is bathing, Deeley confirms to Anna that they have met before. He gives many references from their past about her dress, stockings, white thighs and pubs they frequented, but Kate doesn't say anything.

The play focuses on time and memory. Pinter suggested that memory can operate on a variety of levels. It can offer a fiction that takes on the reality of a fact, especially when Anna describes the London life she had led with the deeply incurious Kate. Pinter loved London, and in part, *Old Times* is a recreation of his own old times. Dilly Hamlett recalls that Pinter sent her a copy of the original script in 1971 with a note saying: "This will ring bells." Indeed it did. Very loud ones. "When I read it," says Hamlett, "it seemed to me to be about our whole milieu in the London of 1950" (qtd. in Billington 218).

Deeley becomes an intruder by marrying Kate instead of Anna. The situation becomes humorous but more ironic. Anna, too, intrudes on the secluded household of Deeley and Kate to gain an advantage. Pinter reveals the conflict throughout the play by using subtle verbal and situational irony. Three characters are placed in separate positions in this triangular relationship. As per the given stage instructions, Anna is positioned in dim light behind Deeley and Kate. She has supposedly not yet arrived. Both husband and wife were peeping into the past to kill time. They indulged in verbal games while waiting for Anna. Pinter depicts that while revisiting the past, the characters remained stuck in the past. Pinter beautifully tunes the fundamental motifs very clearly in the opening verbal combat, where Kate and Deeley discuss Anna even as she stands upstage in semi-darkness. She is clearly present in their imagination even before she appears:

> Kate (*reflectively*): Dark.
>
> Deeley: Fat or thin?
>
> Kate: Fuller than me. I think. (*Pause*) (Pinter, *OT* 7)

The monosyllabic word "Dark" uttered by Kate creates a smokescreen. What does that mean? The room? The situation? The past? Identity? Future? Relations? This word is echoed in outer and inner spaces. In an interview with B.S. Johnson, Pinter claimed that the play is:

> As if the whole thing, then and now, is a kind of very resonant echo in which one moved: an echo chamber, the walls almost of being rubber. One rebounded in echoes all the time, echoes of the sea, echoes of London, the past, echoes of ...colours, if you like, echoes of just things happening, like your tea and your dinner, whatever it was and going to school...Yes, but I say echo, rebound, because there was no fixed sense of being...of being... at all. (qtd. in Batty 93)

The dialogues explore a sense of Deeley's fretful insecurity, Kate's deceptive passivity and their obsession with Anna that runs through the play. The idea that the memories of the past are always provisional, subject to the inaudible process of time, can also be reinvented according to the need of time and power. Deeley revisits the past when he comments:

> Deeley: Was she your best friend?
>
> Kate: Oh, what does that mean?
>
> Deeley: What?
>
> Kate: The word friend...when you look back...all that time.
>
> Deeley: Can't you remember what you feel? (Pinter, *OT* 8)

And when Deeley concludes the argument by saying, "Anyway, none of this matters" (Pinter, *OT* 17), it could mean that any attempt to recover the past is ultimately futile. Pinter shows how the false notion of civilisation is stripped away at the end. Anna is remaking the past and laying claim to prior knowledge of Kate. Steven H. Gale has pointed out that the description of London life is so lively that it exists in her mind either as a vivid memory, as a spontaneous creation or as a combination of the two. Kate recalls her past life in London as:

> Kate: Where artists and writers and sometimes actors collected, and others with dancers, we sat hardly breathing with our coffee, heads bent, so as not to distract, and listened and listened to all those people, creative undoubtedly, and does it still exist I wonder? (Pinter, *OT* 18)

The cracks in their composed memory are exposed when Anna shows up. At first, they seem like an odd pair. Kate is all blonde, serene and remote in contrast to Anna, who is dark-haired, severe, expressive and extravagant in speech and gesture. Yet, something passed between them twenty years ago, something intense and engulfing, making Deeley wonder if he really knows anything about his wife's past or present. While Kate sits still on the white couch, Anna and Deeley civilly battle for her possession. They speak in a comical way, "sing off" where they try to hit

Kate's memory, saying, "They Can't Take That Away From Me" and "Blue Moon" (Pinter, *OT* 27).

The play is not a simple trip into the past, but it has deeper connotations. Every time the past slips away and re-appears with new interpretations, it can be perceived as a tale of interrogation. Past is no longer reachable or might be dead by now, but it is still affecting the present of the characters. Memories, for them, are like the negative prints of the lived experiences that are transforming with the passage of time. Deeley embodies the essence of a lost past as he sings the following lines:

> Deeley sings: When a lovely flame dies...
>
> Smoke gets in your eyes. (Pinter, *OT* 28)

Pinter used a number of techniques in the play to describe the battle between Deeley and Anna and to denote the subjective nature of memory—songs and movies that enrich the texture of the play. At one point, Anna and Deeley engage in a competitive recollection of popular standards from the 1930s to the 1940s. On one level, it is a nostalgic riff; on another, an acquisitive contest in which Deeley constantly caps each of Anna's quotations. Anna says that "we may remember something that never had happened as we recall events they do happen" (Pinter, *OT* 32). Both Anna and Deeley are unsure of the past. They both look towards Kate to validate what happened. The songs, too, are selected carefully to enhance the play's basic theme of remembrance. They show how a smell, a sound or an image from the past unlocks a whole set of emotional experiences. As one can see in the following lyrics:

> Deeley: (*sings*) The smile of Garbo and the scent of roses...
>
> Anna: (*Singing*) The waiters whistling as the last bar closes... (Pinter, *OT* 29)

The song ends in complete silence. Deeley starts discussing the movie *Odd Man Out* that they had seen earlier in London. Now, the real battlefield becomes their shared past. Deeley stakes his territory by telling a cosy story about how he and Kate first met on a hot summer day at a movie theatre showing "*Odd Man Out*" (Pinter, *OT* 29). Anna trumps this memory by saying she and Kate had seen the movie together first. Anna tells Deeley:

> Anna: ...there is something one remembers even though they may never have happened...this man crying in our room...found him sobbing, his hand, over his face...But I would have nothing to do with him, absolutely nothing. (Pinter, *OT* 31)

Act Two is placed in a bedroom, and a bathroom door is made visible. Deelay and Anna's gloves are off, but the battle lines are drawn between them. While Kate is bathing, Deeley brings the coffee and recreates the memories of meeting with Anna twenty years ago in a pub. Deeley and Anna are engaged in an eyeball-to-eyeball confrontation. Deelay recalls the first meeting with Anna at the Wayfarer Tavern and later at a party in Westbourne Grove where he stared up her skirt at her thighs. It is not sure, but many hints suggest that Deeley is creating a past to suit his own needs. Deelay says:

> Of course we met before. We've talked before. In that pub, for example. In the corner. Luke didn't like it much but we ignored him. Later we all went to a party. Someone's flat, somewhere in Westbourne Grove. You sat on very low sofa, I sat opposite and looked up your skirt. Your black stockings were very black because your thighs are so white...I simply sat sipping my light ale and gazed... gazed up your skirt. You didn't object, you found my gaze perfectly acceptable. (Pinter, *OT* 51)

The contest becomes more visible when Deeley indicates that Anna might like to dry Kate in her bath towel. In his review of *Old Times*, Daniel Jeffreys points out that this play is preoccupied with memories as a weapon—especially when a husband and a wife clash over trifles.

> Deeley: Have you dried yourself properly?
>
> Kate: I think so. (Pinter, *OT* 60)

These odd-man-out feelings only increase when Deeley and Anna swap anecdotes about perhaps knowing each other long ago. Deeley relates a story about seeing her at a party and freely looking up her skirt, a tale that becomes disturbing and taboo when Anna informs him that she was wearing Kate's underwear at that time.

> Deeley: looking up your skirt in her underwear. Mmnn.
>
> Anna: But from that night she insisted, from time to time, that I borrow her underwear—she had more of it than I, and a far greater range—and each time she purposed this she would blush, but purpose it she did, nevertheless. (Pinter, *OT* 65)

However, Kate can barely hold on to the memories that Anna and Deeley recall in such detail. She drifts in and out. At one point, she is not even able to pinpoint what tastes she had when she was living carefree, single life in London with Anna. Kate and Anna lived together in London and used to go to pubs and call girls. It also indicates a lesbian relationship between them. But Deeley makes the situation more complicated by claiming:

> Deeley: We've met before, you know.
>
> Anna and I (*Kate looks at him*). (Pinter, *OT* 69)

Here, one can see Pinter's own obsession with past memories. He felt that it was important to bear in mind that "one's memories are completely wrong, completely inaccurate, about everything and this is particularly true of talking about an experience like evacuation" (qtd. in Billington 215). There are things to be remembered that may never have happened, but Pinter declares, "I recall them, so they do take place...great work of art is like a dream: it happens but it does not explain itself and is never unambiguous" (214).The last chilling words of Kate demolish both Anna's friendship and the whole history of Kate's marriage to Deeley. Kate comments:

> Kate: She fell in love with you...you were so unlike others. We knew men who were brutish, crass.
>
> Deeley: But I was looking up her skirt?
>
> Kate: That's not crass. (Pinter, *OT* 70)

The power shifts from the host to the intruder in Act Two, when Kate willfully allows herself to be led down memory lane with Anna. Kate shakes off her statements and takes control, giving her version of the past events that both contradict and complement what has been said before, and suggests that the two friends seamlessly shared identities as well as underwear. Deeley validates their past experiences by recognizing:

> Deeley: If it was her skirt. If it was her.
>
> Anna: Oh, it was my skirt. It was me. I remember your look...very well. I remember you well.
>
> Kate: (*To Anna*) But I remember you. I remember you dead. (*Pause*) I remember you lying dead. (Pinter, *OT* 71)

His sense of entitlement and sureness revoked, Deeley emerges from this evening a fractured man. The sobbing Deeley goes to Anna's divan, looks down at her, moves to the door and returns. He goes towards Kate's divan and lies on her lap. Then, he walks to the armchair where he sits slumped. It signifies that all three characters are locked, like the rest of humanity, into a condition of frozen, permanent solitude. The play ends in full light, very bright—Deeley in the armchair, Anna lying on the divan and Kate sitting on the divan.

At the end of Act Two, Kate narrates another tale by claiming that she remembers that Anna was dead and her face was dirty. She says that her dead body was covered with mud and that the corpse was gone when a man arrived. She told the man that no one slept in the extra bed, and he lay in it, thinking Kate would sleep with him. Instead, she suffocated him with mud from the flower pot by the window in the memory trip, and his reply was a proposal of marriage and change of environment too. This memory trip switches on a number of past experiences at the same time; for instance, Kate is talking about death, dirty face, proper decorum, bath time, sitting, being naked, sexuality, flowers, vases and weddings. It seems as if the memories of the past have been triggered by Anna's arrival, but in the end, the characters are under the control of the memories. There is a flurry of questions that oscillate in viewer's minds who are transported into the mindscape of the characters where the sense of being real or unreal has been blurred. Is Anna really present, or is she simply a figment of Deeley's or Kate's imagination? Are Kate and Anna, who worked as secretaries and shared a London flat together twenty years ago, separate characters or dual aspects of the same woman? Are they using the past to gain power over each other? If yes, then why? Are they cultural products of the aftermath of war? Are they themselves the victims of war? Why do they practice power at home?

Written in 1970, *Old Times* is one of Pinter's most satisfying memory plays, with the careful usage of language and moments of humour. The play on stage is an irrelevant verbal batting between Deeley and Anna for superior knowledge and ultimate possession of Kate. The larger meaning arises from the action about the provisional nature of memory or the essential solitude of human existence. When Mel Gussow suggested to Pinter that New York audiences would inevitably argue about the reality of the events, Pinter succinctly replied, "I'll tell you one thing about *Old Times*. It happens. It all happens." Yes, but what happens exactly? All the memory plays of Pinter are like guided dreams, with their roots in Pinter's own memory. There is certainly something enigmatic about the structure of *Old Times*.

The puzzling statements of the characters about each other and the oddly varying descriptions of past happenings lead to endless interpretations among the characters and audiences too. The play ends, creating a mysterious and hallucinatory framework of memories. The characters return to their positions, Deeley in the armchair, Anna lying on the divan and Kate sitting on the divan, with full bright lights. It ends in modernity, where they know all the facts but are still impaired. The play ends after a hundred minutes in a blaze of bright light, with Deeley slumped once again in the armchair, Anna lying on one divan and Kate sitting on another chair.

The ambiguity lies in the images selected in the play and remains there. Through Anna's character, Pinter has explored a new face of memory and the art of memorising, which is again a political tool and, in a culture, a forcible one too. Pinter does not give *Old Times* a tidy ending, just a blinding flash of what might happen to these three people now that the long-held illusions are shattered. *Old Times* is slightly different from Beckett's *Waiting for Godot,* where Godot never comes and is merely imagined, but the situation remains the same. Estragon and Vladimir are in a dilemma about whether he is present or absent and continuously struggle to authenticate their identities and existence. Unlike Godot, Anna comes in *Old Times*, but her arrival cannot change or bring any change to their fate. Anna's arrival can ignite the past memory or the present situation but cannot change it. It could also be seen as a dramatisation of a fight for a secure territory or sexual advantage among the characters.

It may be Pinter's own Sisyphean search for truth that turns out to be false at the end of the play. He himself believed that everything could be true or false at the same time. Pinter suggests that personality cannot exist without memory, and by usurping others' memories, personality itself is duped or attacked. Lovers reclaim parts of themselves in the enactment of shared memories, be it a film or a party, but what would happen if the events cannot be corroborated? Pinter shows us that characters can be annihilated by being written out of the past while living in their present. Their reality is constantly filtered through an understanding of the narrative of their past.

Like Pinter's other memory plays, *No Man's Land* (*NMN*) is about universal issues of anxiety, insecurity and digging into the past for security. It is a very melancholic play. It is full of gloomy remarks about ageing and helplessness. The characters seem to be crippled, helpless and in darkness far away from civil society. *No Man's Land* is set in a house in North West London on a summer night and the following morning. It has four characters, Hirst, a man in his sixties; Spooner, also a man in his sixties; Foster, a man in his thirties; and Briggs, a man in his forties. It opens with a kind of imprisonment of Hirst in his own house. He is a wealthy man of letters. He meets Spooner, a minor poet, in a Hampstead pub and invites him to his inactive or dead, drink-filled home. The action of the play is full of Spooner's attempts to imperialise Hirst's world, including that of his servants Foster and Briggs, and find a way of establishing himself permanently there. Spooner uses past memories as proof of his European cultural sophistication. For him, the past is a weapon with which he can dominate the servants and situations. He certainly suffers from a neurotic desire to dominate the world and the people around him.

Commenting on the play in *The Sunday Times*, John Peter says:

> It is haunting because it speaks of, and speaks to, the unconscious. Spooner is not merely a down-at-heel poet; he is also Hirst's alter ego, his conscience, his nagging reminder, the painful debit on his spiritual balance sheet. This is why each man keeps recognizing features of his life in the other. Hirst is the king of the mind, arrogant but crumbling: Spooner is the exile of that mind, anxious but tenacious. (qtd. in Billington 245)

Act One begins on a summer night. Spooner stands in the center of the room. He is dressed in a very shabby suit, a dark faded shirt and a creased spotted tie. Hirst is pouring whisky at the cabinet. He is dressed precisely in a sports jacket and well-cut trousers. He offers a drink to Spooner, saying:

> Hirst: As it is?
>
> Spooner: As it is, yes please, absolutely as it is. (Pinter, *No Man's Land* 1)

In John Peter's opinion, *No Man's Land* is an anatomy of the creative life in which success is forever haunted by shabby failure, the public posture by the private anguish (qtd. in Billington 245). Like Pinter's other memory plays, *No Man's Land* is about universal issues of anxiety, insecurity and digging in the past for security. Spooner looks about the room and states:

> Spooner: what a remarkably pleasant room. I feel at peace here. Safe from all danger. But don't be alarmed. I shan't stay long. I never stay long, with others. They do not wish it. And that, for me, is a happy state of affairs. My only security, you see, my true comfort and solace, rests in the confirmation that I elicit from people of all kinds a common and constant level of indifference. It assures me that I am as I think myself to be, that I am fixed, concrete. To show interest in me or, good gracious, anything tending towards a positive liking of me would cause me a condition of the acutest alarm. Fortunately, the danger is remote. (Pinter, *NML* 4)

In Lloyd Bradford Syke's review, *No Man's Land* has a superb characterisation whereby Pinter's trademark linguistic acrobatics, tragedy, comedy and meanness ensue. The taboo of homosexuality perverts all the relationships in the play. Pinter creates an effect of it throughout the play by keeping upper-class standards of hypocritical morality. One is endowed with a keen sense of love-hate in the relationships and tenderness tempered with the pretense of "masculine" cruelty (Syke 2). This tendency develops a powerful undercurrent in the play. Hirst and Spooner may have known each other at the university, and they boast about women they had shared or stolen in a fit of joke. It comes barely out of their apparent likings or disliking. The two men are of a certain age, trying desperately to keep themselves on the safer side, and Pinter portrays them more artistically when he confesses that the "speech is a stratagem to cover nakedness" (Syke 2). It is a kind of consciousness that he has embodied in his characters.

Pinter's plays are about confused, screaming and agonising states of the human mind of the modern man. The important aspects of his plays are the absence of communication, problems of identity, cruelty menace and disturbing existential gnawing torment in mind. In *No Man's Land*, Spooner says:

> Spooner: Experience is a paltry thing. Everyone has it and will tell his tale of it. I leave experience to psychological interpreters, the wet-dream world, I myself can do any graph of experience you wish, to suit your taste or mine. Child's play. The present will not be distorted. (Pinter, *NML* 7)

The guest (Spooner) refills the glasses and thanks Hirst for inviting him, claiming not to want to stay long. He overrides the conversation by speaking English and having poetic expressions. Both start reminiscing about past lives until Spooner asks about his wife, but receives no answer, and then mentions his own. Hirst suddenly rises and throws his glass. Spooner mocks Hirst's meaninglessness and his life. Hirst retorts, saying:

> Hirst: No man's Land…does not move…or change…or change… or grow old…remains…forever…icy…silent. (Pinter, *NML* 22)

He collapses twice and crawls out of the room. Spooner lights a cigarette when Foster enters. Foster repeatedly asks what he is drinking and who he is. Spooner is silent and just says he is a friend of the host. Foster, who introduces himself as Jack, claims that Hirst is his father. Then Briggs enters and asks Spooner the same question. Foster and Briggs mock Spooner that his name is "Friend." Briggs recognises him as a pub employee but, on the contrary, claims that he is a friend of the pub landlord. Hirst re-enters after a nap and brings an album. Pinter uses photographs as a medium to evoke the past. According to the critic Schacter:

> Our memories are not photographic, producing snapshots of the past. Instead, we recreate or reconstruct our experiences rather than retrieve copies of them. Sometimes, in the process of reconstructing, we add feelings, beliefs, or even knowledge that we have obtained after the experience. In other words, we add bias to our memories of the past by attributing to them emotions or knowledge that we have acquired after the event. (qtd. in Winter 3)

Hirst comments on the appearance of the people in the photographs. Foster meanwhile states that Spooner has been claiming to be a friend of Hirst. But Hirst insists that his true friends are kept safely in the album, saying:

> Hirst: My true friend, look out at me from my world. I have it.... We're talking of my youth, which can never leave me. No. It existed. It was solid the people in it were solid. (Pinter, *NML* 35)

Spooner and Foster concretise the past through imprisoned moments in time and Hirst through facial gestures and actions recorded by the camera. It is another proof of their weakness, as they want to fix or define everything according to their own standards, even their past. But with all their nuances of language, descriptions, style and outlook, all three characters yearn for a secure and certain past as a place of protection against the fragmented, discontinuous present.

Hirst begins drinking from the bottle and mutters incoherent speeches, and tries to recall a dream about drowning. Spooner abruptly interjects, saying, "You saw me drowning in your dream. But have no fear. I am not drowned" (Pinter, *NML* 37).

Luccinia Gabbard argued in *The Dream Structures of Pinter's Plays* that *No Man's Land* is one of the best examples of Pinter's dream-like absurd plays. There are a number of elements of dream phenomenology regularly appearing in this play. "The play is a kind of mystery of the working of the human mind itself. Hirst is the possessor of mind and hubris of consciousness and other characters can be viewed as the figments of his own desires" (Gabbard 89). Hirst's dream about drowning can be decoded in Jungian terms, in which water is considered a symbol of the subconscious and for birth and creation. Hirst's repeated description of his dream about the lake where someone might be drowning symbolises the repressed psyche of the particular race or culture. Once again, like *Old Times*, one can see here that the characters are living in the mindscapes as they have been evacuated from the landscapes. In Pinter's opinion, there is hardly any distinction between the real and the unreal.

Hirst collapses again. Spooner rushes for his aid and brushes away the younger men. He claims to be better connected to him because of his age. Briggs and Foster become defensive. Briggs is sent out by Hirst, and Foster laments over Hirst's behaviour. Foster informs that Hirst's financial adviser will come tomorrow. Briggs returns and reveals that Foster is Hirst's housekeeper and he himself is, too, a personal servant. He says:

> Briggs: We're out of bread. I'm looking at the housekeeper. Neurotic poof. He prefers idleness. Unspeakable ponce... He is nothing but a vagabond cock. (Pinter, *NML* 42)

No one can trust these characters because no one can judge who they are and what they are saying. The situation in the play is typical Pinteresque—full of menace, insecurity and anxiety of the modern culture. Two men (Hirst and Spooner) recall their past and suddenly become serious and doubtful about it. As they become more alcoholic, their behaviour also changes. The attitude of Briggs and Foster also changes during the play. The scene ends with the following remarks of Foster.

> Foster: Listen. You know what it's like when you are in a room with the light on and then suddenly the light goes

> out? I'll show you. It's like this. He flicks off the lights, causing a blackout. (Pinter, *NML* 44)

Act Two opens with a cat-and-mouse contest between Spooner and Briggs. The next morning, Spooner gets up from his chair and is ready to leave, but the door is locked. Briggs soon unlocks the door, enters and draws the curtains, asking if Spooner is hungry.

> Spooner: I have known this before. Morning. A locked door. A house of silence and strangers. (*He sits and shivers*).
>
> The door is unlocked. Briggs comes in, key in hand.
>
> Briggs: I've been asked to inquire if you are hungry.
>
> Spooner: Food? I never touch it. (Pinter, *NML* 45)

Since the financial adviser does not reach out, Briggs offers Spooner adviser's breakfast. As Spooner eats and sips, Briggs tells him how he met Foster. It shows how Spooner cleverly wins the present moment. By entering into a competitive memory game about a fantasy, he tries both to secure a position in Hirst's present and in his life. In other words, recollections of the past, even absurd and fantastical ones, can be used as a means of protection from fears and insecurities. They keep talking, keep changing the subject, keep playing games and postpone the terror of death and eternal silence. Hirst is delighted to see Spooner, whom he refers to as an old friend named Charles Whetherby, whom he has not seen in years. When Hirst enters, he immediately begins telling a lie concerning Spooner's true identity. He calls Spooner "Charles" (Pinter, *NML* 55) and speaks of him playing squash, attending Oxford and what role he had played in the war.

They discuss university life in the 1930s and romantic encounters with the same women. In the heat of the duel, Spooner proclaims, "It is you who have behaved unnaturally and scandalously, to the woman who was joined to me in God" (Pinter, *NML* 65). Hirst is accused of having an affair with Spooner's wife. They discuss various faces in the photograph album. Spooner shows great interest in the photo album, but Briggs and Foster discourage it. Pinter creates a transition in several ways, for instance, by stating Hirst's offer to show

Spooner his photograph album. Hirst's poetic imagination of ghostly figures in the photographs is easily personified into life to show sympathy for the living,

> Hirst: Deeply, deeply, they wish to respond to your touch, to your look, and when you smile, their joy...is unbounded'; to the pragmatic, ruthlessly undercutting Briggs: They are blank, mate, blank. The blank dead. (Pinter, *NML* 68)

But the absolute change in the play seems impossible as the only change we witness in terms of physical actions, like the fading of lights, drink cabinets and closing of the curtains, Hirst points out the following:

> Hirst: The light...out there...is gloomy...hardly daylight at all...Distasteful. Let us close the curtains. Put the lamps on...Ah. What a relief how happy it is. (Pinter, *NML* 75)

Spooner again refers to poetry and ignores Hirst when he asks why the door was locked. Spooner claims he must be out for a meeting. Then, Briggs mentions that Hirst and Foster are poets. Spooner, adept in the duel memory game, jumps right in without missing a beat. He knows how to play the game. However, he does not know how to win. In the fight against exile, the men use language as a game. Spooner uses language forcefully by rarely allowing his host to speak. He uses language to create a power he really does not possess. Saul Bellow once stated that powerlessness appears to force people to have recourse to words. Spooner played the ditto game, but memory constantly shifts to adapt the strategic moves in the verbal chess game he plays with Hirst. In the process, it becomes extremely difficult to sift the real past from the modified memory.

Hirst feels privileged and praises himself for his work ethic. Suddenly, he changes the topic. The most critical departure in the game occurs when Spooner says, "Let me live with you and be your secretary." Hirst replies, "Is there a big fly here? I hear buzzing" (Pinter, *NML* 78). Spooner, too, wishes to be appreciated for his past, age and experience. Yet Spooner and Hirst are cast aside, and their wisdom is ignored. Hirst speaks of his past life as though it was filled with afternoon teas, a wife, a daughter and a country home. Later, Spooner's tone changes as he babbles out a lengthy monologue, boasting over his triumphs and blunders, praising Hirst's talents being a poet. Spooner pretends to be clever in his arguement, and Hirst remains silent during Spooner's display of knowledge about Hirst. Spooner no longer has any claim, and his dispassionate advocacy of Hirst is badly ignored in the play. Spooner finds his common battleground with Hirst but sabotages the companionship by asserting superiority over his host. Spooner raises his status by asserting his superiority, and Hirst proceeds to reassess his purpose in visiting his home. It leads him to the revelation that if Spooner were to join the household, he would be as domineering as Foster and Briggs. Spooner informs Hirst of his needs, hoping them to be fulfilled and thus achieving his own desires. He says:

> Spooner: I ask you...to consider me for the post. I was one of the golden of my generations... I will accept Temperamentally. I can be what you wish. My character is, at core, a humble one. I could read the Bible to you. I am a good companion... I will accept death's challenge on your behalf. (Pinter, *NML* 79)

Hirst and Spooner argue with their supposed memories throughout the play. MacGeever wrote that Spooner undercuts his chance to achieve a home through his own manipulations. Spooner insists on a degree of respect not only for himself but for Hirst too. In the case of Spooner, the stake is high as he deals with basic human survival. The men seek a roof over their heads and food in their bellies. However, Spooner needs companionship and a purpose in life. Spooner is in a desperate fight. He constantly tries to boost his image at the expense of others. Spooner is fighting to be granted the respect his age and experience deserve instead of becoming entombed in insignificance. Spooner's age is the reason for his rejection at the hands of much younger characters (Foster and Briggs). However, it is Spooner's demand for respect and for Hirst to achieve dignity that causes Spooner's exile. Spooner, being a jailer, asks Hirst to do what he fears the most to live again. He comments in the last section of the play:

> Spooner: You would be there in body. It would bring you to the young, the young to you. The elderly, also, those who have almost lost hope. (Pinter, *NML* 81)

The final shift in the play is towards a living death, an engraved deadness from where memory is exiled forever. Hirst's desire for the active present is reflected in his act of asking Spooner to read his poem in the upstairs room of a pub. But the silence that follows this request is articulated in the following exchange of words:

> Hirst: Let us change the subject. (Pause)
>
> For the last time. (Pause)
>
> What have I said?
>
> Foster: You said you're changing the subject for the last time.
>
> Hirst: But what does that mean?
>
> Foster: It means that you'll never change the subject again…if the subject is winter, for instance, it'll be winter forever…spring will never come. (Pinter, *NML* 83)

With Foster and Briggs in charge, Hirst can slip into insignificance and just stop living. Spooner cannot reinstate his zest for life and significance that would enable both men to live out their days in relative happiness. Hirst thinks back to when he sees a drowned body in a lake, and says:

> Hirst: Yes. I am walking towards a lake. Someone is following me, through the trees. I lose him, easily. I see a body in the water floating… I look closer and see I was mistaken. There is nothing in the water. I say to myself, I saw a body, drowning. But I am mistaken. There is nothing there. (Pinter, *NML* 85)

Hirst first acknowledges a memory and then denies or negates its possibility. By doing so, he also denies the possibility of change in his life. Both Hirst and Spooner seem to have reached an extreme point where they have been locked in the fixity of no man's land, which, as Spooner reminds us, forever remained icy and silent. As the play concludes, it appears that Spooner has failed and that Hirst has finally entered into a kind of living death—a spiritual and physical no man's land. Spooner tries hard to rescue himself from this deadness. Spooner admits that Hirst is now in that solitary, icy wasteland, as the title of the play suggests. In Spooner's words, "You are in no man's land" (Pinter, *NML* 86).

In a way, Pinter was seeking a philosophical answer to the question of existence. He is successful in his task of pointing out that under the surface of comedy lies a bleak recognition of the fact that the entire humanity is trapped inside its own skin, either corporal or social and that all of them occupy some undefined space between past and present, birth and death, security and fear. Spooner comments, "No, you are in no man's land, which never changes. And the lights fade slowly to black." In Martin Esslin's view, Pinter presents:

> A symphonic structure of variations on the theme of betrayal that, ultimately, becomes an inquiry into the inextricable web of lies that constitutes the social relationships. (qtd. in Scolnicov 2)

In Pinter's case, it is all the more interesting that his plays are memory triggers of his own past experiences designed by him. The play *Betrayal* is inspired by Pinter's own extramarital affair with BBC television presenter Joan Bakewell, which spanned seven years, from 1962 to 1969. The play is set in London and Venice from 1968 to 1977 (in reverse chronology). The first thing to notice about *Betrayal* is its title; a rather startling abstract noun that appears without either a definite or an indefinite article. This lack is especially noticeable in the context of many other Pinter titles that carry the definite article, such as *The Room*, *The Birthday Party*, *The Caretaker*, *The Dumb Waiter*, *The Collection*, *The Lover*, and *The Homecoming*, as well as *A Slight Ache*, with its indefinite article. The omission of the article indicates that the topic is the idea of betrayal, its generalised or abstracted structure, and not the story of one particular instance of betrayal (Scolnicov 2). However, the development of the events and the dialogue is highly naturalistic but extremely supportive of the various plot elements of betrayals.

Pinter universalises the situation so that people who see the play come out saying, "Oh! It's the story of my life." The play comments on the emotional insecurities of men and women in married life. *Betrayal* involves three characters in a romantic triangle. In *Betrayal,* Pinter has created nine symmetrically arranged scenes like a series of interlinked betrayals—disloyal marriage, lovers' strange sense of truth, male companionship and literary idealism. In the investigation of a seven-year long affair between Jerry and Emma, Pinter leaves no aspect of betrayal untouched. Pinter's art showcases that a dramatist should be a maker of actions in the play, not a man of action. As a result, his works are, in a sense, transmutations of his and his people's personal experiences. To a large extent, Pinter's play *Betrayal* captures his own anxieties, fears and obsessions as well as those of European culture. Pinter, too, concurs:

> I think every writer does that one way or another. Otherwise, what are we writing about? What we write has something to do with ourselves, and observable reality about us. We're not writing about the moon. But I think as long as the work is written with understanding, it is legitimate. I'm not using words like "compassion," because that is not what drama has to do…in *Betrayal* I think the situation that a wife finds herself in is one which a lot of people will associate with…It's situation you find yourself in and what do you do about it? You live it and you find your ways out…this is life… What can I say about *Betrayal*?… I did that. (qtd. in Billington 258)

Undoubtedly, Pinter deals with extra-marital relationships, but the important question that arises—who is the actual person being betrayed in the play? Scene One is set in 1977 (Spring). In a pub, Emma and Jerry meet for the first time in two years. For seven years, they had an affair and a secret love nest. Emma is also having an affair with Casey, an author. Jerry is an agent of Casey, and Robert (Emma's husband) is his publisher. Emma says she found out last night that her husband has betrayed her with other women for years and admits that she revealed to Robert her affair with Jerry. He (Jerry) has betrayed both Robert and his own wife, Judith (unseen on stage). Judith is having an affair with a doctor. Emma has betrayed not only Robert but also Jerry by not disclosing to him that her husband found out about the affair five years ago. Robert has also betrayed both Emma, through his own serial adultery, and Jerry, by not letting on that he knew about the affair.

Pinter's characters are the product of self-contradictory cultural forces. They hang in between instinct and reason. They are denizens of the competitive modern world where winning love and wealth is the prime motive for their existence. For such a sense of victory, they all are constantly cheating upon each other and are willing to be cheated by others as well. They use the past to win or betray. Scene One begins in a pub. Emma is sitting at a corner table. Jerry approaches with drinks and sits. They smile and toast each other silently. He looks at her, and the conversation begins with these remarks:

> Jerry: Well...
>
> Emma: How are you?
>
> Jerry: All Right.
>
> Emma: You look well.
>
> Jerry: Well, I'm not at all that well, really.
>
> Emma: Why? What is the matter?
>
> Well, it's nice sometimes, to think back. Isn't it? (Pinter, *Betrayal* 13)

They recall the past through the act of narration, which is a social phenomenon, and are completely transported from the past into the present. Here, one can see that past events are becoming more prominent and alive than the present. Emma remembers the happy memory of playfully throwing up the baby (Charlotte) in the air by Jerry. This can be seen as a classic example of a momentary incident that can be turned into a dramatic and cultural metaphor. Emma recalls it as follows:

> Emma: Do you remember that time...oh God it was... when you picked up and threw her up and caught her? (Pinter, *Betrayal* 19)

Jerry remembers the emotional moments, and Emma recalls the precise circumstances. Both have their own sensibilities over the same past moments. Here, one can see the act of remembrance and how this act of remembrance varies. Remembrance is definitely a social act, a personal memory that is not necessarily a cornerstone, but it is always shaped and reshaped by all social factors. Jerry continues with the memory thread, saying:

> Jerry: Yes, everyone was there that day, standing around, your husband, my wife, all the kids, I remember.
>
> Emma: What day?
>
> Jerry: when I threw her up. It was your kitchen.
>
> Emma: It was in your kitchen. (Pinter, *Betrayal* 20)

Jerry and Emma have now become the denizens of a memory-filled world. They seem to be living in the golden past (full of love). Jerry comments:

> Jerry: Oh! Love finds a way...
>
> Emma: We were up...all night.
>
> Jerry: But he's my oldest friend, I mean I picked his own daughter up in my arms and threw her up and caught her, in my kitchen. (Pinter, *Betrayal* 29)

Emma turns him down in the memory game by concluding:

> Emma: It doesn't matter. It's all gone... It's all over.
>
> She drinks. (Pinter, *Betrayal* 30)

The time is unidirectional and so is the plot of this play. But from the perspective of memory, all stories are terminated processes, viewed from the vantage point of the present, so that unfolding a series of betrayals in reverse temporal order may experimentally be the more natural procedure for Pinter. The reverse chronological order eliminates the memory-related discrepancies that abound in other plays of Pinter.

Jerry meets Robert to talk about the affair in Scene Two, which takes place at Jerry's house (later during the same day). Robert reveals that he had already learned about the affair four years ago. The friendship between Jerry and Robert continues, albeit without playing squash. In a conversation, they discuss whether Emma had told Robert about her relationship with Jerry:

> Jerry: As she told you...last night...about her and me. Did she not?
>
> Robert: No, she didn't tell me about you and her last night. She told me about you and her four years ago. So she didn't have to tell me again last night. Because I knew. (Pinter, *Betrayal* 38)

Arthur Hugh Clough has pointed out that behind the play's actions lies aching awareness of how the high ideals of youth are betrayed by the compromises of daily life (qtd. in Billington 258). Jerry, a married literary agent, had a love affair with his best friend's wife, Emma, for seven years. This love affair is full of common trappings, like stolen afternoons, secret love nest and its destiny and pains too. Behind the mask of civility, the play is actually full of lies and deceits played upon each other.

Linda Benzvi is of the view that Pinter provides all the identity data to the audience so that it may gain a complete grasp of the past of the characters. But it seems that the playwright is mocking his audience, suggesting that the mystery of the human personality remains elusive, also unchanged. Scene Three opens in a flat in 1975. Ironically speaking, it is the end of Emma and Jerry's affair in the play. They rarely meet, and Emma's hopes that their love nest would be a different kind of home are still unfulfilled. So, they agree to give up. They are shown on the stage as if in the present, but the dialogues take place in the past tense. Through the reversal of time, Pinter has also created a threatening disillusionment about love and marriage (Scolnicov 3). It opens a game of betrayals, which are an inevitable part of human nature. The relationship between time and memory has been shown in reverse chronological order. This technique emphasises the absurdity in the play as the audience and the characters are unable to locate themselves in time and space. Emma's dialogue depicts an oscillation in the given time-space continuum:

> Emma: You see in the past...we were inventive, we were determined, it was...it seemed impossible to meet... impossible...and yet we did. We met here, we took this flat and we met in this flat because we wanted to. (Pinter, *Betrayal* 52)

The characters pretend to end the affairs, but this is not the end of betrayal, as it leads to another riddle in the next scene. Scene Four is set in the living room of Robert and Emma's house in 1974 (Autumn). Jerry visits Robert and Emma at their place. He discloses that Casey has left his wife and is living nearby. Jerry and Robert plan to play squash, but Jerry reveals that, first, he would be visiting New York with Casey. The actual structure of the play thus appears to depict a repetitive pattern of multiple betrayals. Enoch Brater defines such a structure as having the influence of the filmic technique of the flashback where the past has been subjected to an 'objective' point of view, a cinematic technique wherein the characters remain enigmatic and unfathomable (qtd. in Benzvi 235).

Scene Five takes place in a hotel room in 1973 (summer). Robert and Emma are on a holiday, intending to visit Torcello the next day. Emma is reading a book by Spinks, whose agent is Jerry. Robert says he refused to publish it because there is not much about betrayal in it. Robert has discovered that Emma has received a personal letter from Jerry. Emma admits that she is having an affair with Jerry. Emma announces that while Jerry was in America, she became pregnant with Robert's child. Emma has a beautiful style and her own unique way of betraying too. Her recollection is more vivid, and her character is more powerful than that of Jerry. However, Pinter does not suggest that she is emotionally secure—she is still shocked and hurt after knowing of her husband's infidelity the previous evening. But Jerry seems more shocked than Emma by the news of Robert's clandestine affair.

The theme of the play is the corrosive complexity of betrayals and the mess of our emotional lives. Emma's revelation that her affair has been going on for five years is followed by Robert's italicised "*Five years*?," which suggests a mixture of emotions—incredulity, indignation and anguish. It is frequently followed by Robert's question about the paternity of their one-year-old son Ned. Emma's assurance that Ned was conceived while Jerry was in America leads to an extraordinary exchange:

> Robert: Did you tell him that Ned had been conceived?
>
> Emma: Not by letter.

> Robert: But when you did tell him, was he happy to know I was to be a father?
>
> (*Pause*)
>
> I've always liked Jerry. To be honest, I've always liked him rather more than I've liked you. Maybe it should have had an affair with him myself. (Pinter, *Betrayal* 86)

Hanna Scolnicov has observed an element of ego-centricity or neurotic tendency among lovers that acts as an antidote to love (5). They neither care about others enough nor are prepared to give something up for each other. The middle-class institutions of marriage and family groups internalise the supreme values, and love affairs are merely a sidekick for both parties, who do not invest too much in them emotionally. The multiple betrayals consolidate infidelity as yet another bourgeois institution, and in this context, the affair is divested of any rebellious, heroic or glorified proportions and is ironical. The irony of the characters' life is that though they have many pleasurable sources to fill the void, they are emotionally isolated—even when happily married. Emotional isolation is the tragedy of modern culture—a threat to one's self at home. Marc Silverstein states:

> We can only fully grasp the political resonance of the power struggles in Pinter's plays if we see the question of who will occupy the dominant position within the marriage as inseparable from the larger question of whether the family will serve as a stable site for the articulation of patriarchal power or as the vanishing point that works to undermine that power and the cultural order it supports. (qtd. in Batty 66)

Scene Six takes place in a flat in 1973 (Summer). Emma has returned from the holiday with Robert from Venice. She has bought a tablecloth for the flat. Jerry reveals to Emma that despite having an affair with her, he continued to have lunch with Robert.

> Emma: No, I mean why are you taking him to lunch?
>
> Jerry: Because it's my turn. Last time he took me to lunch.
>
> Emma: You know what I mean. (Pinter, *Betrayal* 95)

Robert gets drunk over lunch with Jerry in Scene Seven, which occurs in a restaurant in 1973 (Summer). Robert says that he visited Torcello. He also hates modern novels and brandy, which stinks of modern literature. He claims that he is a bad publisher. He criticises modern prose because it forces a kind of judgment and promises on his part for money.

> Robert: I am a bad publisher because I hate books... I mean modern novels...all that promise...falls upon me to judge, to put firm's money on... Waiter! Another bottle of Corvo Bianco...it's worse in Venice...they really don't give a fuck there. I'm not drunk... I hate brandy...it stinks of modern literature. No look, I'm sorry. (Pinter, *Betrayal* 116)

Robert, being a publisher, becomes a character who is the product of self-contradictory cultural forces. *Betrayal* seems to infect and undermine the fabric of human relations. The old religious and social restraints that gave rise to a sense of sin or guilt and demanded punishment, jealousy, outrage and revenge have been replaced by a more civilised and urbane containment within the accepted norms of society. In this kind of educated, western, yuppie society, the idea of *Betrayal*, which forms the nucleus of the play, has been refined into a self-obsessed contemporary society. Scene Eight happens in a flat in 1971. Emma wants to know whether Jerry's wife suspects an affair. D. Keith Peacock points out:

> All human interaction is inherently political is to dilute the field of what constitutes political writing to meaningless extremes but if Pinter's writing has often dealt with behavioral strategies adopted in the face of oppressive cultural forces then, it has to be recognized that his ambition has been more sophisticated than simply to represent that human interaction. (qtd. in Batty 67)

In any case, tracing Pinter's interest in political issues only by his plays is a myopic approach that cannot speak for Pinter's stance as a citizen (67). Pinter's writing has often dealt with behavioural strategies adopted in the face of oppressive cultural forces. Then, it must be recognised that his ambition has been more sophisticated than simply representing that human interaction. The acceptance of infidelity is devoid of moral censure and hurt.

Scene Nine takes place in Robert and Emma's bedroom in 1968 (Winter). During a party at the house, Jerry surprises Emma in her bedroom and declares her love for her. In an interview with BBC in 1960, he said, "In contemporary drama, so often we have a villain, the society and the hero, the individual. These two things—the man in relation to society—exist and one makes the other. Society wouldn't be there without the man, but both are dependent on one another and there's no question of a hero or a villain" (qtd. in Billington 81). One can observe such a situation in Jerry's case particularly. He tells Robert he is his oldest friend as well as his best man, and Robert, too, confesses in the end:

> Jerry: I was best man at your wedding. I saw you in white. I watched you glide by in white.
>
> Emma: I was not in white.
>
> Jerry: You know what should have happened?
>
> Emma: What?
>
> Jerry: I should have had you, in your white, before the wedding. I should have blackened you, in your white wedding dress, blackened you in your bridal dress, before ushering you into your wedding, as your best man.
>
> Emma: My husband's best man. Your best friend's best man...
>
> Jerry: I speak as your oldest friend. Your best man.
>
> Robert: You are, actually. (Pinter, *Betrayal* 138)

It is not the end of *Betrayal*, but the origin of many kinds of betrayals. In other words, memory, language and creativity also betray on a much bigger scale or maybe life, existence and identity itself is a form of betrayal. This play is also full of nostalgia for the past and the irony of life and relations. Past, which is no more than a "still memory," carries its own traces toward the future.

The characters are quite opaque in their intentions to dominate or win the situation in the play. Scolnicov has opined that the daring time reversal of its plot has settled down, and the artistic edges of the work can be seen more clearly. One can see the supremacy of the play's abstract shape over its narrative content and its grip on the relevance of time with memory. The play is dispassionate and ironic in tone, and it deliberately avoids a moral stance (Scolnicov 1). The chronological reversal is instrumental to this general shake-up of the dramatic form and style. The characters' constant search for meaning is shared by the reader or spectator but deflected through the sophisticated formal shaping elements used by Pinter. The play is an experimentation with a presentation of human relationships in terms of game sequences. It explores the duality of human lives in reality and in minds that run parallel to each other. The play also suggests that memory and creativity are too deceitful, like language.

Drama as a genre in itself is an act of remembrance and memory process. Pinter has achieved the heights of this process in his memory plays, especially in *Old Times*, *No Man's Land* and *Betrayal*. Human beings are nothing but a whole summation of their past memories. By telling and retelling the past tales, they want to authenticate their existence and identity. For the characters, the act of memorising means filling the gaps in between the narration, searching for identities, which are in dynamic relationship with the present life of the characters, and depending upon the playwright's power of narration. Who, when and how can one narrate one's tale of life is politicised by the power of the state through narration. It means identities are created by the power of narrative-like history, which is one form of past or identity.

Ironically, Pinter's *Old Times*, *No Man's Land*, *Betrayal* and other memory plays show an anti-authority proclamation of people's past or identity. The character's obsession with memory is basically their craving for lost identity, space and existence. The plays reflect Pinter's own longing for a Jewish identity, which was badly injured in war trauma and tortured during the Jewish Holocaust. It also creates questions, like "Are his characters purely Jews, fighting for their identity in modern world through personal memory trips?"

Pinter deals with human isolation and the crucial problem of communication through the characters' attempt to recall the past. All these plays have a static quality and signify mental paralysis. The struggle for power is intertwined with everyday life, full of invasions and intruders who threaten life and start a battle for territory. The ever-changing nature of memories and the temporary hold of characters over truth and reality open up a more insecure world in which the desire for security, command and communication is definitely shattered. Memory always carries with it the present-ness of the past, present-ness of the present and present-ness of the future. We can see how the memory-making process can be legitimate and plays a vital role in identity formation, as Harold Pinter's memory plays clearly establish.

Pinter's characters can move, grow old and change, but the icy land they have acquired or perhaps have been thrown into remains eternally fixed. They cannot escape from this given situation. No doubt, they may have a chameleon-like tendency to change and also have kaleidoscopic visions, like poets using brilliant expressions of language. Pinter painted such menacing nakedness of human (Jews) existence from *Old Times* to *Celebration* successfully. In order to cover the menace of existence, Pinter and his characters try hard, but the situations always engulf them. Being a great artist, Pinter manages to escape these situations through the process of re-creating them. But being an involved citizen, Pinter strives to keep the truth of human oppression at the centre stage. His political pronouncements target those who abuse power and manipulate language to keep those truths obscured. Through his plays *Old Times*, *No Man's Land* and *Betrayal*, Pinter has shown a cultural sterility due to powerful oppression over all kinds of human interactions. This oppression has created a kind of emotional paralysis. In his own unique way, Pinter deals with the aftermath of World War II and the Holocaust.

3
Inheritance of Cultural Memory

Harold Pinter's extraordinary analysis of the workings of the human mind and its memory processes revealed the ability of human beings to connect everything from a remote past to an accessible future. In Pinter's corpus, memory is a method by which human beings represent and transform their past experiences. His characters are living in a memory-filled world where the past dwindles in their minds and hinders their present actions. For his characters, the act of remembering becomes a mere mechanical utterance. The characters are repeating the past and seem incapable of carrying the burden of inheritance. The whole drama of one's past memories depends upon the ownership and inheritance of a traumatic past.

The outlook of twentieth-century Europe was designed by the haunting memories of war and the Holocaust. The engraved experiences and traumas of the war became a narrative type in European culture. War experiences challenged human knowledge about memory and its ability to sustain itself. Whenever inheritance seems to be a big failure, it transforms into frustration and rage. For Pinter's characters, when a lost past is inherited as it is, without knowing, its need in the present and the future is deformed. The plot of life stories thus became a kind of regression rather than resistance. War memories and shared pasts were owned by people either by choice, ignorance or, at times, through forced inheritance. Pinter's characters are not listening to or speaking with each other. Their communication is not linear, nor do they indulge in any one-to-one correspondence in the plays. The characters have created a symbolic commotion in society rather than communication.

War memory is full of echoes of the past. It resonates all the time throughout generations, as Pinter has showcased in his plays. History speaks through the language of its particular people, as one can see in Pinter's plays. He used absurd language as a tool to open up the locked doors of history using the archives in the form of words, sounds, images and silences. Memories are the texts of a particular historical event and are produced by a keen engagement with that event. Without memory, experience has no meaning, and the consciousness would be frozen in the present moment. In Pinter's works, the documentation of the Holocaust has come out as a collapse of the truth and identity of the characters. "Who am I?" becomes the most important, painful and absurd question in the play and both the characters and the playwright combat with it. In other words, the process of identity formation is revised through a notion of history, which is not only unconventional but also assumes a non-linear, discontinuous, non-chronological and anti-authoritarian representation.

The memories are carried forward from generation to generation through a tradition of a culture. Culture is understood in and through the contents of its traditions. Tradition carries the feelings, modes of action, forms of language, aspirations, interpersonal relations, images and ideas of a social group. They project the personal and communal experiences of the people through their art forms, myths and stories. The emotional core of the social group is developed and sustained through traditions. Inheritance happens through the traditions of the people and depends upon the very act of narration. The narration needs public acceptance and articulation in the social group as well. When narratives are accepted in social spheres, they become revolutionary and bring more fruitful changes to society. The narratives grow in the social arena through negotiations and anchor the people more firmly by creating healthy relations among people.

The knowledge of the whole lived past is stored in the form of traces. Cultural memory contains both the history of the people and the memory of the people. The contribution of Jan Assmann and Aleida Assmann to have seen the whole literary world within the frame of cultural memory and introducing the term 'cultural memory' remains unsurpassable (Winter 117). Cultural memory is a narrative that directs and organises lived experiences and makes it sensible to continue the grand narrative of the human race. Cultural memory also explains the power structure to the people. The cultural memory can be said to reside in those fissures, gaps and silences or in the residual elements where the history could be said to deconstruct itself. The connectivity between past and present is possible through technologies and the fashion of commoditisation in modern times. In the age of mass production and mass consumption, traumatic past objects have repeated past events without any kind of emotional value. For the inheritance of cultural memory, it is mandatory to rescue the witnesses of the past for future generations. In such cases, one is not only creating anti-history through historical reconstruction but also preserving the reservoirs of social or personal memories. Cultural memory becomes:

> As important as a survival mechanism, when it becomes a part of artistic and emotionally laden ways of forming group identity and meanings suggested. The very basis of human knowledge is the outcome of finely tuned emotional structures. (Rodriguez and Fortier 2)

Revisiting the past had become a creative phenomenon for Pinter. He has shown the past through empathy in his plays and recreated the past as a useful source for life and art. The present and the future can never be isolated from the past. The dialogue between past and present is very much productive for the future. Art forms played a very important role in this process of the inheritance of cultural memory, particularly war memories.

Life is not a random terrain of events, images and ideas. One's present identity is not a sudden and mysterious incident but an outcome of a well-plotted life story/history. Human beings play a vital role by knitting life stories that make them unique from other creatures. Connerton suggests that in every mode of experience, man always base particular experiences on a prior context in order to ensure and understand it. "The world of percipient, defined in terms of temporal experience, is an organized body of expectations based on recollections" (qtd. in Connerton 6). Before any single experience, the human mind is already occupied within a framework of typical shapes of experienced objects. One can perceive an object or act upon it and locate it within a given system of expectations. Man has always based the particular experiences of the past to ensure the present experience, which makes it intelligible in the present context. The world could be understood through the prism of past experiences. Whenever a social group makes a desperate effort to create something new, it seems to be an illusion of illusions because the beginning has nothing new to carry forward. The traces of past recollections are always present in all the beginnings, and simultaneously, beginnings also carry traces of the past, willingly or unwillingly. It is basically the occurrence of a metamorphosis of past lived experiences that shape memory.

Memory is a social practice and lies at the core of human societies. Social groups provide individuals with frameworks within which their memories are localised and memories by a kind of mapping. The collective memory cannot exist without any reference to a socially specific spatial framework. The images of social spaces provide the illusion of stability and also imagine a secure future. Therefore, man started rediscovering the past in the present. Human beings position what they recollect within mental spaces provided by social groups. Hallbwachs insisted that the mental spaces received support from social groups. He says, "Our mental equilibrium is, first and foremost, due to the fact that the physical objects with which we are in daily contact change little or not at all, so providing us with an image of permanence and stability" (qtd. in Connerton 37).

Human beings are always mentally indulged in reconstructing the past for the present and future. And the past is always inherited with social and cultural conditions. The act of memorising the past supports the cultural and social institutes of life through various communication tools, such as gossip, newspapers, telephones, radio, films and art forms. They are the major factors that shape daily memory and history. Communication tools also preserve memory and history in a more productive way for the future. Being a powerful narrative form, daily gossip also plays a very crucial role in society. It is a highly personal as well as political tool to fill up the gaps in the human narrative. Gossip includes the memory as a faculty, the practice of remembrance and the social phenomenon of inheritance of cultural memory. The inheritance of memory or the past is not as simple as it looks. It exists in the unconscious mind (in the form of traces), but consciously, it is a matter of ownership.

One may recall or evoke the memories in day-to-day life through one's direct or indirect relation with their social group. One is able to remember something because others stimulate them to remember, and it becomes a communal act in which the individual feels that he is participating. The memory of a social group needs the aid of individuals, and the memory of individuals finds support in social groups. Even the unexpressed thoughts and sentiments of an individual person survive in a strong relationship with their social group. The groups also have automatic consent to carry forward the lived past that one can observe in the languages of the people. The language embraces the said as well as unsaid experiences of the people. Language also includes people, places, dates, words, forms and images; that is, the whole material and moral life of the societies we are part of. In the context of cultural memory, it is a people who carry "a memory and the memory in itself is also the carrier" (Rodriguez and Fortier 7). Rodriguez further states:

> Memory is transmitted is through narrative. Narrative emphasizes the active, self-shaping quality of human thought. Its power resides in its ability to create, form, refashion, and reclaim human identity. It is the narrative that explicate to people, their deeds, beliefs, fears, anxieties, trends as well as the whole living apparatus. (Rodriguez and Fortier 7)

Past events have a deep impact on what we do and how we, even coming generations, will live in the future. In any culture, it is that social group that carries the particular memories for future generations. Every time, a powerful social group chooses a fruitful memory bank for future generations. Memory, in itself, is such a powerful tool that it can carry itself even through fissures, silences and gaps in the narrative order.

In the European context, the difference between social memory and the historical reconstruction of the past in the form of monuments and museums is upheld as an essential requirement to understand Jewish history. Ortega y Gasset said, "Man, in a word, has no nature; what he has is...history" (Hinchman and Hinchman 163). History is constructed partially from the accounts of witnesses who were involved in the historical events both as victims and onlookers and partially from the records that documented the events. The act of historical reconstruction is a reincarnation of the actual events with all cultural facts that are always influenced by particular perspectives. The historical reconstruction of the war memory is deeply influenced by the surroundings and survives in the form of images, symbols, ceremonies and rituals that seem to be even more convincing than actual events. Historical memories are transmitted through texts, oral history, tradition, plays and memory. However, historical reconstruction becomes mandatory when the social memory has been silenced or erased. Social memory becomes evidence of the occurrence of the Holocaust in Europe. One can see in the European context that historical reconstruction and social memory were totally dependent upon each other. In a particular case, the state apparatus was used in a systematic way to deprive its citizens of their social memory. The German totalitarians were keen to erase the memories of the chosen events. They had gained psychological control over people and their sentimental subjects. With the passage of time, the transmission of the whole lived experience became an important phenomenon, a contested territory.

One may simply consider memory as an individual faculty, but some critics do believe that it is a collective or social phenomenon. The tradition of telling and listening to different stories needs validation. Through the act of negotiation, the social groups provide space, validation and authenticity to the act of narration. These groups can either be small units or larger communal systems. In a social group, individuals learn through various practices, the sense of identity, unity and meaning of life. But a particular social group carries particular memories for future generations. It means it is the dominant social group every time that chooses the powerful memory reservoir for future generations. One of the most complicated aspects of memorising the past is that it is always absent, and its effect cannot be eliminated. It runs traditionally with all kinds of possible strictures. According to Connerton, there is a huge difference between past and present recollections at a psychological level. He states:

> Of bringing the past into the present: "acting out and remembering". Acting out includes the action, with the grip of unconscious fantasies and it affects the present actions. It appears in the form of refusals, betrayals and aggressive behavior of the characters. This kind of behavior could be against others or against the self too. But in compulsive repetition the character has forgotten the present situation and behaves in a 'caught-up' situation. (Connerton 25)

One can see Pinter's characters often repeat rather than recall the past. The past of the characters in the plays overrides the present actions and does not allow them to act normally in the present condition. Here, one can see that the act of remembrance has failed. As a result, remembrance becomes pure repetition. Neurotic patients repeat their actions rather than recall the past. They are actually in a caught-up condition.

Social groups always select healthy memories for a better future. People never choose painful past events like the Holocaust, except for mourning ceremonies, especially those people who have really experienced war traumas. Memories are located in the mental and material spaces of social groups. Connerton said:

> Society tends to eliminate from its memory everything which could separate individuals' or that, at certain moments, 'society is obliged to become attached to new values, that is to say to depend upon other traditions

> which are better relation with its needs and present tendencies. (Connerton 38)

Painful memories have their own life span. Such memories have the capability to block the other spheres of memory and remembrance and disrupt the act of inheritance. It can paralyze, but in extreme cases, it is fatal. Culturally inherited memories tell people who they are and what their identity is. But war memories are infected, diseased and disabled. These are not fit for daily narration in life. These memories are disjointed, quick-sand in nature and totally incoherent. The more tightly one tries to hold on to them, the more quickly they slip away. How such memories can create a coherent identity or self needs to be examined. Such dormant war memories are located in the mental and material spaces of social groups. So, society tends to eliminate from its memory the drastic events that could disperse its individuals. At such crucial moments, society is obliged to adopt new values too. To cement all individual bricks of the social group—people forget or are forced to delete painful memories that can destroy the course of life.

The formation of a fixed human identity germinates from memory as a narrative. The tremendous power of memory distinguishes man from other creatures. Man always carries the traces of the whole lived past through memory. The way one can perceive past events affects one's present situation. Cultural memory cannot be understood in isolation or apart from the social frame of a particular social group. People's memories are inherited through their narratives. However, the narrative is blurred in structure. It contains the trans-subjective truth of the people and their lives. It also offers perceptions about the world around and gives validation to the lived experiences. Societies and their present existence largely depend upon the remembrance of the past and their ability to retain the past. A society organises and interprets the reality of the world to its people through a successful narrative order.

The unique aspects of narrative discourse enlighten people by interpreting their stories through different methods of telling and retelling. The contemporary life of both the individuals and the members of the social group are chalked out by the contours of the past and aspirations of the future. The reality is conceptualised through the narrative framed by the culture. Lewis and Sandra Hinchman suggested that memory is the storehouse of the narratives. They elaborated that memory is culturally and traditionally transferred by the social groups in their social, historical and political contexts. The social context includes all modes of communication among people. The historical context contains the history of the people and the historical reconstruction of their past events. In the political context, memories are raised through celebrations, rituals and mourning acts. In culture, the memory of a social group is sustained through the process of inheritance. A social group chooses collective memories that they want to pass on consciously and traditionally. In the seminal text *Memory, Identity, Community—The Idea of Narrative in the Human Sciences*, the role of narrative in the formation of identity and community is described in the following manner:

> Narratives, then, are what constitute community. They explain a group to itself legitimate its deeds and aspirations, and provide important benchmark for nonmembers trying to understand the group's cultural identity. (Hinchman and Hinchman 235)

The tale of the twentieth century cannot be narrated without reference to the traumatic memories of the wars and the Holocaust. The image of the furrows of the battlefields in Europe has been sustained in the minds of the people. The exile of civilians and soldiers from their home, forcible evacuation and break in the continuum of daily life were the unique features of wars. Hitler's Nuremberg Laws in 1935 deprived the German Jews of citizenship and all civil rights. Innumerable laws had been passed to exclude Jews from mainstream society. Nazis wanted to achieve supremacy through the purity of blood and its rootedness in the German earth. Jewish intellectuals were the first to withdraw from the war scene.

Walter Benjamin left for Paris on March 18, 1933. Albert Einstein visited the US on January 30, 1933, and declared that he would never set foot in Germany again. The people who experienced particular threats, like war, were in a rage, and their memory processes refused to act according to the given situation. The haunting images and experiences of war disturbed the narrative of the personal lives of both the onlookers and the victims. The orderly sequence of the lived experiences was broken up due to drastic conditions, like disease and death in families. It could not be balanced against the chaos, and as a result, the life course was suspended. The daily narration filled the gaps between the past, present and future. In Europe, five million people became victims of an endemic disease, *Encephalitis Lethargica* or sleeping sickness. It was a sense of living in a state between sleeping and awakening. In the aftermath of the war, one-third of the affected people died of it since a drug called L-DOPA that could cure it was not available.

According to Pinter, though the survivors had escaped death, a majority had moved into a state of deepening illness. Pinter wrote in the introduction of the play *A Kind of Alaska*:

> Of the survivors some escaped almost unscathed but the majority moved into states of deepening illness. The worst-affected sank into singular states of 'sleep' -conscious of their surroundings but motionless, and without hope or will, confined to asylums or other institutions. Fifty years later, with the development of the remarkable drug L-DOPA, patients erupted into life once more. (Pinter 151)

The horrible features of war experiences were stored both in the bodies of the victims and of the victimisers. Pinter's characters were telling through gestures what they had done or seen. Here, one can see the exact caught-up situation in which they repeat the past rather than recall it. Pinter subtly creates deranged body movements on the stage through his characters. The futile effort of a man to stand up, to walk out of control or to be unable to coordinate the body properly also became one of the war stories. The tales people shared with each other defined them—who they were, who they are and who they would be in the future. In this way, the narration completed the circle of their life course. The victims and onlookers both suddenly journeyed back to the primitive standards where a man was a beast (or had no sense of being human) and where memory was full of mere gloom and darkness. Pinter's characters were caught in such a past—where memory comes and goes intermittently whenever they got stimulated. According to Connerton:

> The war experiences seemed ironic in design with a dynamic hope for future and were crucial for the reconstruction of the past. It is phenomenal to imagine for the members of two different groups (Victim and Onlooker) participate in the same event, which was so catastrophic and all-engulfing. (Connerton 20)

The war memories estranged the victims during the act of narration. Both the victim and the onlooker can scarcely be said to refer to the same event. One of the best examples suggested by Connerton is that of Carlo Levi. He was exiled in 1935 as a political prisoner to the remote village of Gagliano in Southern Italy. On the wall of the town, a marble stone was inscribed with the names of the dead people who had lost their lives during the war. However, during Levi's discussions with the villagers, he found that they had no concern with war or the dead and their sufferings. They talked about the war of brigands that had taken place in 1865 when brigands had fought with the army and the government. They negotiated it, gave a mythic coherence and the hues of the war of brigands. The story of the war was not, a part of their lives (Connerton 20). It was not taboo to remember the war and its pains. Nobody was ready to fess up.

Here, one can notice how the act of inheritance had become a challenge for them. The past narrative relates to the self of the individual and to society. In his fictional and philosophical chronicle, *The Man Without Qualities*, Robert Musil speaks through his main character Ulrich, suggesting that the narrative order is: "...the simple order that consists in one's being able to say: 'when that happened, then this happened'." Ulrich goes on arguing and describes that:

> In their basic relation to themselves most people are narrators. They do not like the lyrics or at best they like it only for moments at a time. And even if a little

> "because" and "in order that" may get knotted into the thread of life, still they abhor all cogitation that reaches out beyond that. What they like is the orderly sequence of facts because it has the look of a necessity, and by means of the impression that their life has a "course" they manage to feel somehow sheltered in the midst of chaos." (qtd. in Hinchman and Hinchman 188)

Memory had social and political connotations. For example, the storage of present-day records in indexes and data collection are not merely a technical process. In fact, it basically satisfies the hunger for validation, control and ownership because people want to know what they were, what they are and what they would be in the future. Man's identity evolves with the passage of time and past experiences. Thus, he takes more interest in rediscovering the past in the present context and imagines a secure future. He is always capable of mentally reconstructing the past for the present and future through the act of narration. However, in Europe, the personal and social dialogue was absent in the framework of the twentieth-century narration. The very personal act of narration was not supported by social or relational narration, as seen in the context of Pinter's characters. Unfortunately, for war-like incidents, people could not afford negotiations. They were under threat even when they had to talk about such human conditions to themselves. People scared of looking back in the past ironically recalled Osborne's *Look Back in Anger*, but Pinter dared to look back and also into the future. Human beings situate what they recollect within mental spaces provided by social groups. These mental spaces receive support from social groups. A personal narrative is well-knitted and preserved in a social group's narrative from where the personal gets identity and authenticity. Social groups provide individuals with frameworks within which their memories are localized.

Joshua Solomon wrote in *Living the Holocaust* that World War II was over in Europe on May 7, 1945. But for the survivors of the Holocaust, the war remained within them for the rest of their lives. War had stripped them of their identity. The trauma took away even the very sense of being human. They came to realise that their families would never reunite or return to them.

All their efforts to achieve normalcy in life failed. The memories of the concentration camps and the shock of separation from their loved ones reverberated in their minds. The war memories caused a radical change in mental behaviour to such a degree that it took the form of survivor's syndrome (Joshua Solomon 1). The symptoms seen in survivor's syndrome would normally be seen in a typical patient with post-traumatic stress disorder. The psychological imprint of the disaster, anxiety and guilt appeared in their behaviour. The personality changes germinated in the rearing of the children of the survivors. The children were astonished to observe why their parents were not like other adults who did not have tattooed numbers. The victims and onlookers suffered from different forms of personality changes, behavioural quirks and obsessions. They began to feel that a sense of sharing the past had become a repeating mechanism rather than a remembrance.

In his plays, Pinter has revealed all the stages of human memory, including the crisis of inheritance as well. Pinter was not poor on dates and names. He had an extremely powerful, lively imagination with accurate emotional hues. He portrayed modern man's struggle with traumatic war memories. His characters constantly fight with the past. He practised well in the process of the inheritance of cultural memory, even if it was a traumatic one as the Jewish memory. Pinter's war memories were full of exiles, loneliness, bewilderment, forcible separation and loss. The war themes and scenes repeatedly recur in his works, especially in *A Kind of Alaska* and *Moonlight*. His parents were Jewish. They were imprisoned and separated from their only child. As a child, for Pinter, separation from parents was approximately equal to death. The rare meetings were full of pain and followed by heart-wrenching departures. Pinter's parents, Jack and Frances, could not afford the rail fare to Cornwell. When they had come down to Cornwell, they were highly emotional, and there were tearful farewells. "On one visit," Pinter recalls:

> When they left to get the bus it was a long way back to the lodge for me to walk. But I went all the way to castle and looked back and could just see them as pinpoints waiting for bus on the road; and I suddenly ran all the way back to them over the mounds of grass, racing

> towards them and of course they came towards me too. (qtd. in Billington 67)

As Billington points out, "This image was lodged in Pinter's memory. In these circumstances, Pinter also became aware for the first time of the low cunning *Lord of Flies* like cruelty of the boys in isolation he said: "I think as a result of that loss and confusion are became, generally speaking, nastier, just horrid is the world. I think we were all a bunch of horrid little boys because of the loss of security" (qtd. in Billington 67).

For a genius like Pinter, the play *A Kind of Alaska* (*AKA*) had become the epitome of memory loss during World War I (1916–17). *A Kind of Alaska* was inspired by Oliver Sack's *Awakenings*, which was a medical study of twenty patients who were the victims of sleeping sickness. The play is a reincarnation of the particular case study of Rose R by Oliver Sack. Rose R was the youngest kid of a wealthy family in New York. The case study is full of social life descriptions, like parties and aeroplanes. Rose was a victim of sleeping sickness for forty-three years, and Sacks cured her with L-DOPA. He recorded her surprising awakening: Her songs, jokes, mannerisms, speech regression and nostalgia. Oliver Sack, who is an expert neurologist, said about the play that it "is just like truth."

The play is based on the case histories of a strange time-stopping disease called sleeping sickness. *A Kind of Alaska* is a one-act play written in 1982. In this play, a middle-aged woman, Deborah, has been suffering from sleeping sickness for the last thirty years. Suddenly, she awakes with the mind of a sixteen-year-old girl. She confronts the body of a middle-aged woman. It seems to have aged without her knowledge and consent. Deborah emerged from a mysterious state between life and death. The setting of the play in a comfortable sitting room is deceptively normal. The play opens with Deborah lying in a contorted position on a bed under a lace coverlet. A man named Hornby sits by her, silently observing her. Then, he asks:

> Hornby: Do you know me?
>
> Do you recognize me?
>
> Can you hear me?

> Deborah: Are you speaking? (Pinter, *A Kind of Alaska* 154)

Deborah stirs and murmurs. She is half awakened. Her consciousness is suspended in animation without a means of self-expression either through action or through voice. With the aid of medicine, she has sprung into life once more. Deborah experiences complete isolation from the present world of her sister and Hornby. She does not know what has been happening around for the last twenty years. Pinter exactly scans the brain waves and their broken rhythms through words, tones and subtle projections through Deborah's character. Deborah was frozen in the past at the age of sixteen. She speaks excitingly about her sister's marriage and her future like a teenager.

> Deborah: Is Estelle going to marry that boy from Townley Street? The ginger boy? Pauline says he's got nothing between his ears.
>
> Hornby: She didn't marry him.
>
> Deborah: Didn't? (*Pause*) It would be a great mistake. It would ruin her life. Hornby: She didn't marry him. (Pinter, *AKA* 159)

Pinter subtly paints a dream-like structure of Deborah's life where three time entities—past-present-future—co-exist, but she cannot connect them. It appears more absurd and intense as the play moves on. When Deborah sees her younger sister, who has now become a middle-aged woman, she reacts strangely:

> Deborah: Well you have changed...A great deal. You've aged...substantially. What happened to you? (Pinter, *AKA* 178)

What Deborah means is that her sister has not only changed physically but is a different person now. The two worlds of the past and the present co-exist but cannot meet in the play. It seems absurd and painful. Not only the characters are helpless but the audience is also equally crippled. Deborah is astonished to see the corporal changes in her sister's outer appearance. She exclaims:

> Deborah: Are you my sister? ... But where did you get those breasts?

Pauline: I am a widow.

Deborah: This woman is mad. (Pinter, *AKA* 182).

Debora's remarks are not absurd but tormenting. She seems to be indifferent as well as concerned at the same time while dealing with the situation and the people around her. She does not know about her past life and is unable to understand the present situation. In fact, she is being informed by Pauline and Hornby about the whole past thirty years. Pinter empathises with Deborah, who, at the age of forty-five, suddenly awakens from sleeping sickness after twenty-nine years. Through Deborah's personal troubles with the connectivity of past-present-future, Pinter triggers the frozen past memories between the conscious and the unconscious worlds. He reveals the act of memorisation and inheritance in a given society.

Deborah, the sixteen-year-old girl, who suddenly wakes up in the body of a forty-five-year-old woman, intensifies the situation in the play. Sitting up in the hospital bed where she has been lying for thirty years, she seems as fragile and insubstantial as a shadow or a spirit. When she asks whether something is happening, her voice is as light and innocent as a child's. It is surprising, too, how a melodious voice comes out of a middle-aged woman. Pinter creates a new lyricism in absurd drama through the characters' mental states. They were speaking what their minds perceived. They were so threatened that they coiled themselves in their minds. Pinter had worked out in the play to make words cut as deeply as the silence. He used words and silence to explore the character and his past. Pinter revealed the spaces between the words, those who feared silence in which characters stepped back and reflected on whatever lies they had just spoken.

The distance is unachievable between the two worlds; that is, one of Deborah's world and the other of Pauline and Hornby's world. One can see Deborah as the denizen of the past and Pauline and Hornby as the dwellers of the present. These two different worlds are visible in their way of talking as well. It also explains to the audience how past experiences can validate the present and the future. In the social construction of memory, the past plays a vital role. Hornby confirms in the play what actually has happened to Deborah in the past twenty-nine years. She re-awakens to a changed world, and this changed world is introduced to her by Hornby as one introduces the old-world tradition to a newborn. It is a direct reference to the social construct of memory and identity formation. It includes the basic act of inheritance as well. The act of inheritance seems a natural social phenomenon in the existing world. Hornby introduces Deborah's sister, saying:

> Hornby: This is your sister. Your father is blind. Estelle looks after him. She never married. Your mother is dead. It was I who took the vase from your hands. I lifted you onto this bed, like a corpse. Some wanted to bury you. I forbade it. I have nourished you, watched over you, for all this time. (*Pause*) I injected you and woke you up. You will ask why I did not inject you twenty-nine years ago. I'll tell you. I did not possess the appropriate fluid. (*Pause*). You see, you have been nowhere, absent, indifferent. It is we who suffered...your mind has not been damaged. It was merely suspended it took up a temporary habitation...in a kind of Alaska. (Pinter, *AKA* 184)

One could say that it is maybe Pinter, not Hornby, who is present here and trying hard to save Deborah as a memory. Pauline's husband, Hornby, was Deborah's doctor and a devoted doctor for over three decades. Hornby might have fallen in love with Deborah, which appears to her to be a rather more shocking revelation. The inherited irony among the characters, situations and their life is that they tried hard to achieve the equation, but it is the only thing they could never afford. All of them were caught in their given situations.

Separation, which was an inseparable part of the war memories, is very difficult to express in words—the pain growing out of this predicament is really threatening. The question of human existence becomes more haunting. War memories unveil the memory game more clearly and define human time/life as a complete waste. One can see in the play how the lives of the three characters have degenerated during this course:

> Hornby: Your sister Pauline was twelve when you were left for dead, when she was twenty I married her. She is a widow. I have lived with you. (Pinter, *AKA* 185)

The play showcases the absurdity of life. The characters are spectres of the fractured arts of modern times. All characters are running through psychic sores as the situation is slipping away from their reach. Deborah's awakening intensifies the tragic fates of all other characters. The play ends with an ironic observation about her sister and brother-in-law that can only go so far toward accepting the realities that they have allowed her to know. Deborah reports back from imprisonment in an ever-shrinking chamber of mirrors where walls are deceptive windows. It is the actual Alaska where the mind can never stay but is just cheated upon by illusions. Deborah says to the doctor that there is something shady about the situation:

> Deborah: Let me out. Stop it. Let me out...shuttering the walls on me...so tight...with enormous interior windows masquerading as walls. The windows are mirrors, you see. And so glass reflects glass. Forever and ever. (Pinter, *AKA* 189)

Pinter has created a beautiful contrast in Deborah's character where the past and the present co-exist. But she cannot connect her past with the present along with the other two characters. Both past and present are equally important for her and her future, but the tragedy is that she can never connect it. The plot of her life has been fragmented. Her last words are still mysterious in tone and cannot afford any reality. Deborah utters:

> Deborah: She [Estelle] is a widow. She doesn't go to ballet classes anymore. Mummy and Daddy are on a world cruise. They've stopped off in Bangkok. It'll be my birthday soon. I think I have the matter in proportion. Thank you. (Pinter, *AKA* 190)

The disconnected passage of time and memory is thus revealed in Deborah's speech. As the other characters, she too, hangs in between the gaps. The fissures have occurred due to lack of communication, distractions and clogged memory processes in their personal and social scenarios. The play has exposed the hidden areas of the human mind and its workings. One can understand that the act of remembrance can be disrupted by a severe illness. *A Kind of Alaska* is set in a family frame, but this frame is severely fractured due to the illness, *Encephalitis Lethargica*. Deborah's awakening is like a flickering flame of hope in her history, and the whole play is more like a warning against human isolation and failure to connect (Billington 285). Preserving individual memory is essential for ensuring a composite, but not a collective, version of the truth.

As a consequence, the personal becomes political since the individual plays a role in the foundation of truth and the dissemination of power and control. "The removal of power structures is achieved completely in *A Kind of Alaska* as the individual [Deborah] is wholly isolated from other characters and society" (Garner 7). Naomi Garner reviewed in *Politics of Pinter* that the loss of memory (narrative) allows the characters or the situation that can be misinterpreted and accounted for by those arbiters of truth, who can then record the incident according to their own agenda (7). This kind of isolation, separation and deprivation actually happened during the Holocaust and war times. Social apparatus failed, including memory as a narrative, which is the foundation of human identity and its survival. The end of personal or social memories meant the death of a self, which can be considered a new form of birth.

The play deals with unvoiced thoughts and feelings. Sometimes one's personal memories perform resistance by negating cultural or social codes, like loss, death, disease and wars, which are too difficult to absorb and to be passed on to the next generations through silence. Deborah is in complete isolation but is not independent. She cannot modulate her voice to achieve control. Her isolation signifies an absence of the self rather than the presence of the self. For Garner, the presence of the self and the voice of the independent individual is the source of power and control throughout the play. The play is focused on the usage of the language and varied tones of each age group. The result that comes out is mesmerising.

The process of inheritance seems to fail in such drastic social conditions. In the Holocaust-like situations, memory was unable to pass on from personal to social and even political levels. Memories could be manipulated according to the need of time and space to locate identity or to negate what happened in the past. Among war memories, the memories of the Holocaust are dangerous enough for public negotiations and ethnically are unable to travel into the future. They are stored in dormant forms through technology (photographs, films, memorials, autobiographies, biographies and newspapers).

The forcible separation was among the main themes of the wars and the Holocaust. It was a separation from the home, relations, family, lovers and from the self. Jews were imprisoned in concentration camps and estranged from themselves. They were deprived of selfhood, identity and language. They had lost the sense of truth. A stage had come when there was nobody to carry forward the burden of the brutal acts. There was no sense of being inherited with humane and civil features. Life was more like a threatening dream where mere ghost-like characters (Bridget in the play) roamed around or had been awakened by somebody else's past, as Deborah was awakened by Hornby. The awakening was really a painful, festering sore of the Holocaust. There was no one to inherit the past or the experiences of the Holocaust.

In *Moonlight*, Pinter shows the emotional gaps among family members from various angles. In the play *Moonlight*, the stage is divided into three segments, each of which is a different room belonging to a house. In one, Andy, an ex-civil servant, lies dying in bed with his wife, Bel, beside him; in another, also on a bed, are his sons, Jake and Fred; and in a third space above them is their sister, Bridget, who is probably dead and has a ghost-like appearance. The play has three main playing areas—Andy's bedroom (well furnished), Fred's bedroom (shabby) and an area where Bridget appears, through which Andy moves during the night.

The patriarch Andy lies in his bed and is very rude to his wife Bel. His two sons have shown no interest in his situation. Bridget tries to bridge the gaps between youth and old age, life and death. She is an embodiment of a cosy past history of the family life. In the opening prologue, she utters a monologue,

> Bridget: I can't sleep. There's no moon. It's so dark. I think I'll go downstairs and walk about. I won't make a noise. I'll be very quiet. Nobody will hear me. It's so dark and I know everything is more silent when it's dark. But I don't want anyone to know I'm moving about in the night. I don't want to wake my father and mother. They're so tired. They have given so much of their life, in fact. All their energies, and all their love. They need to sleep in peace and wake up rested. I must see that this happens. It is my task. Because I know that when they look at me they see that I am all they have left of their life. (Pinter, *Moonlight* 319)

Bridget appears in dim light on stage. She exists in her own world. Pinter said to his director David Leveaux, "I have a feeling Bridget is dead" (qtd. in Billington 339). Her opening speech on stage seems quite ghostly solicitude. Her speech is full of emotional craving of the dead for the living (339). Pinter immediately shifts the scene to bedridden Andy and Bel sitting nearby. Bel is embroidering, a symbol of domestic fabrication full of emotions, closeness and manipulations. Andy's rage is born out of nostalgia, his longing to connect with family and his unwillingness to leave the home or family. The rage is really heart-wrenching and exposes the emotional ties in the play.

Moonlight is full of emotional hues among family members. Andy, who is on the deathbed, is recalling his early days. Andy, the hero of this play, a civil servant, is dying. He can be compared to the other angry patriarchs of Pinter (like Hirst in *No Man's Land* or Max in *The Homecoming*) whose powers are failing or being challenged. Bel dutifully attends to him, but there is too much awkward chemistry between them. He feels adequately nursed at home, where comfort is offered to him, and he receives it willingly. At the last stage of his life, he constantly tries to connect the two distinct worlds of life and death. He is lustful and has betrayed his wife. Andy's attitude towards his family is full of rage, and his questions to Bel about their sons are quite interrogating in tone:

> Andy: Where are the boys? Have you found them?
>
> Bel: I'm trying.
>
> Andy: You've been trying for weeks. And failing. It's enough to make the cat laugh. Do we have a cat?
>
> Bel: We do.
>
> Andy: Is it laughing? (Pinter, *Moonlight* 320)

Bel seems an indictment of passivity and passive memory. She is unable to find the boys in the play, which means that she cannot support the social memory and the act of inheritance as well. She could not help Andy to bequeath the past. Not only Andy, Bel and Bridget but also his sons (Fred and Jake) are helpless to balance the equation in the play. Bel feels so helpless that she diverts the topic and makes it more humorous for the audience. She personifies the cat as a family member and someone who has the right to mock her. It reveals Bel's own fear of space:

> Bel: She's laughing at me. At my ineptitude. At my failure to find the boys...to their father's deathbed...
>
> Andy: Is this a joke? My God, she's taking the piss out of me. My own wife on my death-bed. She's as bad as that fucking cat. (Pinter, *Moonlight* 321)

In the conversation between Andy and Bel, there are distinct echoes of *Old Times*, *No Man's Land* and *Betrayal*. The joking between Jake and Fred is a pared-down Pinteresque language game. The familiar themes abound, such as "the subjectivity of memory, the impossibility of ever knowing anybody else, the gap between the certain present and the uncertain past, plus the verbal piss-taking humour" (Ghilardi 9). The play's humor starts with the title *Moonlight*, which is ironic. The play combines the concrete with the mysterious. This makes it an extraordinary play. Ghilardi said that Pinter deals with "the subjectivity of memory, the strangeness of one's lifelong partner, the gap between the present and the past and extends his territory" (9). The use of the word territory is particularly apt and suggestive, referring to the characteristic fight for the territory of Pinter's works.

The characters are unable to bear the ruthlessness of life. Bel faces scorn and derision throughout the play. Andy comments: "What a woman you were" (Pinter, *Moonlight* 321). The use of past tense intensifies the situation and the question of survival. Pinter's famous metaphor for past-present-future is marriage, again redefined here after *Betrayal*—marriage is a present relation based on the past and moving towards the future. It is an act of life where we all try to connect three different, isolated entities of time or life together. Like other memory plays, it is not mere digging in the past but rather a hook on with the future through the present. The characters' past affects their present life verbally and non-verbally. Andy immediately dwindles on the other side of life, which is culturally anchored, full of faith and logic. He mocks at it and says to Bel:

> Andy: Rationality went down the drain donkey's years ago' and hasn't been seen since. All that famous rationality of yours is swimming about in waste disposal turdology. It's burping and farting away in the cesspit for ever and ever. That's destiny speaking, sweetheart. That was always the destiny of your famous rational intelligence, to choke to death in sour cream and pigswill. (Pinter, *Moonlight* 322)

Fred and Jake sit in the shadows, speaking enigmatically and cynically, revolving around the fact of their estrangement from their father. Fred and Jake were rationalising love-hate relations with their father, Andy. They find themselves at a distance that they are unable to cover, even when their mother attempts to call them home. They make fun of the serious situation by conversing with each other. One can see in the following remarks how they also ignore the seriousness of the situation and take it casually:

> Jake: It's very important to keep your pecker up.
>
> Fred: How far up?
>
> Jake: Well...for example...how high is a Chinaman? (Pinter, *Moonlight* 324)

Andy's sons Fred and Jake are obsessed with the inactivity and are undergoing a kind of mental paralysis. They consciously isolate themselves from their father's condition but unconsciously remain threatened inside their skins, like Stanley in *The Birthday Party*. Through the verbal game, they are projecting the future. Andy, will leave his fortune for them. In Jake's words, his father's speech is as follows:

> Jake: ...was the speech either of a mountebank—a child —a shyster—a fool—a villain—
>
> Fred: Or a saint. (Pinter, *Moonlight* 332)

The boys are not talking about the real situation and the real Andy. They, too, are probably cementing past-present-future. The idea of Andy, their father, is full of shifts that are disconnected like a dream. While Andy and Bel are unable to bring their sons to their father's deathbed, the couple is visited by old friends Ralph and Maria. Maria remarks: "Do you remember me? I was your mother's best friend" (Pinter, *Moonlight* 332). Her entry makes the situation more intense in the play. She is an old family friend and might have been a lover of Andy. She remembers Andy in a different way, recalling how he danced, and she finds it really funny:

> Maria: How he danced. One of the great waltzers. An elegance and grace long gone. A firmness and authority seldom encountered. (Pinter, *Moonlight* 333)

Her memories of young Andy are more refreshing and sensual in comparison to those of Bel. Her memories are also in contrast to the present situation of the family. A remarkable contrast runs throughout the play between what they were and what they have become now. Pinter subtly painted this contrast on stage. He created a dream-like world where past-present-future co-exist and try to connect. It creates a sense of ever-present nostalgia or seems like an anger of the whole human race. It heightens the pathos and absurdity of Andy's life in the play. By delaying the thoughts of death, Andy himself is expecting the future in the form of another spring. He is aspiring and says:

> Andy: I sometimes think I'm married to a raving lunatic! But I'm always prepared to look on the sunny side of things. You mean I'll see spring again? I'll see another spring? All the paraphernalia of flowers? (Pinter, *Moonlight* 335)

Pinter plays with memories throughout the play and interrogates them as well. Pinter undermines it, restores it and expands the themes of memory's echoes in the play. *Moonlight* is neither quite light nor quite dark, and it's the limbo between life and death, past and present, faith and unbelief that the bedridden Andy occupies. Bel's description of Andy's past is twofold: one is the soft corner of his heart, and the other is full of harsh realities of life. Or maybe Bel finds herself to be a victim of Andy's self-contradictory nature, victim and victimised at the same time. Bel reacts to Andy's remarks and creates a sharp contrast to Andy's tone:

> Andy: Yes, it's quite true that all your life in all your personal and social attachments the language you employed was mainly coarse, crude, vacuous, puerile, obscene and brutal to a degree. Most people were ready to vomit after no more than ten minutes in your company. But this is not to say that beneath this vicious some would say demented exterior there did not exists a delicate, even poetic sensibility, the sensibility of a young horse in the golden past of our forefathers. (Pinter, *Moonlight* 335)

The play is a symbol of rage and failure because, throughout the play, the characters cannot connect the past-present-future or the life-death-life cycle. The entire human existence faces a threat and loss. The bitter truth of separation and isolation is really tragic in the play—whether in relations or between the living and the dead. Characters are stitched inside their skins, masks or roles given to them. They are actually thrown into being, and there is no escape for them. The drama of existence is merely a false attempt to find a hole for escape. "What may not be said in words we must pass over in silence and one of those moments? You must not complicate it: simply suggest the imprint of past on the present" (qtd. in Ghilardi 12). Pinter created Bridget as a figment of the dead past, but she was not buried there. She is not static but moving, restless like past memories in the human mind. She cries, "I am walking slowly in a dense jungle" (Pinter, *Moonlight* 337).

David Leveaux says the title of the play is a pun. Moonlight means the light that appears after sunset or complete darkness.

It signifies the dormant phase of characters' lives between light and darkness and Andy's state of being in between life and death (qtd. in Billington 342). The family has become a battlefield where the emotional game of power is being played. On the surface, the conversation is very humorous throughout the play, but one may find how the same person and the same past can be variously owned by everyone in the play. One can observe this situation in Andy's character. Andy explained the dark secret fears of Pinter's characters and the whole human world. *Moonlight* shows obsession through the repeating thoughts of life and death. One can see it as Pinter's own fear of death, the play's dialogues exchanged between the dying Andy and his wife Bel. The dialogues seem even more poignant because Andy and Bel are angry as well as comic at the same time:

> Bel: Darling, death will be your new horizon.
>
> Andy: What?
>
> Bel: Death is your new horizon. (Pinter, *Moonlight* 357)

In *Moonlight*, if the past is foggy and obscure all the time, so is the future. In fact, the future is pitch-black forever, not only for Andy but for the whole of humanity. Andy finds this situation more threatening and cannot dare to imagine it. Andy mourns, saying:

> Andy: I don't believe it's going to be pitch black for ever because if it's pitch black for ever what would have been the point of going through all these enervating charades in the first place? There must be a loophole. The only trouble is, I can't find it. (Pinter, *Moonlight* 358)

Moonlight is framed by a prologue and epilogue delivered by Bridget while the whole stage is bathed in moonlight. The play is full of fissures, gaps, silences, fractured family structure and a particular kind of separation that exists among family members. The milieu in the play is really aching and creates many emotional ripples. Andy, during the search for whisky, unknowingly enters Bridget's world and feels her presence in the moonlight. Bridget, who is a ghostly character in the play, has her own isolated zone on the stage. One can see it as Andy touches death or glimpses of the dead. The play has a hallucinatory framework throughout.

Andy cries, "Ah darling. Ah my darling" (Pinter, *Moonlight* 360), revealing the sickness of living for dead or reverse too. Jake and Fred are also trying to delete the hurdles of time that separate the whole family. At this level, the communication among characters has become crippled. Jake says about his father, "...he loved me. And one day I shall love him. I shall love him and be happy to pay the full price of love," which, according to Fred, is, "the price of death" (Pinter, *Moonlight* 367). In an ambiguous setting, the character calls up their vague, indistinct memories.

The inheritance of memories or past is not as simple as it looks because the basic nature of memory is to be selective. No doubt it exists in the unconscious mind in traces, but consciously, it is a matter of ownership. Bel's description of Andy's past is twofold. One is the soft corner of his heart, and the other is full of harsh realities of life/world. The dichotomy can be observed when Andy says:

> Andy: I'll never forget the earliest and loveliest days of our marriage. You offered your body to me. Here you are, you said one day, here's my body. Oh thanks very much, I said, that's very decent of you, what do you want me to do with it? Do what you will, you said. This is going to need a bit of thought, I said. I tell you what, hold on to it for a couple of minutes, will you? Hold on to it while I call a copper. (Pinter, *Moonlight* 376)

Andy's daughter (wraith-like) Bridget, roams alone in the faint light; she's a sweet girl devoted to her parents but unable to reach them because she is frozen in time at the age of sixteen when she died. Children are absent, and there is no sign of grandchildren. Andy is briefly visited by a couple of old friends, Ralph and Maria, but derives no consolation from it, despite Maria having been his (and Bel's) lover and Ralph, a good guy. Andy seems to have had an affair with Maria, who may have had an affair with Bel. Bel recalls the past and blushes:

> Bel: The first time Maria and I had lunch together...I asked her to order for me...she took my hand and squeezed it and smiled and ordered for me...she asked about my girlhood.

Andy: The bitch. (Pinter, *Moonlight* 372)

The role of Maria and Ralph in the play is peripheral, but it does allow Pinter to satirise the inanities of middle-class idiom, as when Maria talks of having moved to the country. She elaborates:

> Maria: We have a pretty rundown sort of quite large cottage… We've made friends with so many cows. (Pinter, *Moonlight* 377)

Besides this, Bel has failed to bring about what Andy most wanted—the chance to see his children and grandchildren before he dies. In two separate parts of the stage, Pinter's stage directions specify three different playing areas. In one, Andy's grown-up sons Jake and Fred exchange heartless banter, much of it about the father they're estranged from, and when Bel telephones, in the hope of summoning them, they pretend she's called the wrong number: "Chinese laundry?" (Pinter, *Moonlight* 382).

When Bel calls them, they pretend and refuse to own the situation. Jake replies that it is Chinese laundry. There is a rejection of the whole lived past, of love, emotional ties in family and any expectation for the future. One can say that both the ownership and inheritance of the past or the memories have failed here. The response of the sons toward their father projects a lack of responsibility for the future. When Bel enters their room, Jake transfers the phone to Fred, and one can see the rage in his indifferent tone rather than emotion. It shows a clear-cut denial—both the characters refuse to carry the ownership of the father-and-son relationship in the family unit. They also refused to inherit the whole lived past.

> Jake: Of course we do dry cleaning.
>
> Of course we do dry cleaning
>
> Bel: What kind of fucking laundry are you if you don't do dry cleaning? (Pinter, *Moonlight* 382)

By having strong cultural concepts, like dealing with the family structure and the emotional ties among family members, *Moonlight* remains a mystery or an enigma till the end. The audience or the reader seems in a dilemma about what exactly is going on in the course of the play. Andy inquires on their behalf:

Andy: 'What's happening? (*Pause*) What is happening?'

Bel: 'Are you dying?'

Andy: 'Am I?'

Bel: 'Don't you know?'

Andy: 'No. I don't know. I don't know how it feels. How does it feel?

Bel: 'I don't know.' (Pinter, *Moonlight* 384).

In the end, the situation becomes more paradoxical. Andy is under the illusion that his daughter Bridget and future grandchildren are outside the door. Jake and Fred imagine a memorial service for de'Orangerie. Fred says, "I loved him like a father" (Pinter, *Moonlight* 386). The unique elements in *Moonlight* are the heart-wrenching emotions expressed in Andy's anger and terror at approaching death, the presence of death in life, and the poetic, symbolic nature of Bridget's monologue in the end. Ghilardi considers it as the epistemological role of Bridget in the play for recalling or repeating Pinter's own past. He explains:

> It is a work that doesn't yield all of its meanings easily or lightly especially insofar as the epistemological status of Bridget is concerned to the play's themes recall many of Pinter's yesterdays: here is the old crisis of failed communications; people do not speak; they run talkative circles around each other; family life is a cluster of tensions and schisms; an erotic triangle is lyrically remembered; memory seems just a game people play. The sheer banality of this elucidation of Pinter's intertextuality is a direct result of Pinter's own laboured imitation of his old great self. (Ghilardi 6)

Bridget recalls a family invitation in the dark, and the whole house is soaked in the moonlight. They all move into their imaginary futures. Bridget's manner becomes more poetic in the end. She recites:

> Bridget: I got dressed in something old and I waited for the moon to go down. I waited a long time. Then I set out for the house. The moon was bright. (Pause). When I

> got to the house it was bathed in moonlight. The house, the glade, the lane were all bathed in moonlight. But the inside of the house was dark and all the windows were dark. There was no sound. (*Pause*). I stood there in the moonlight and waited for the moon to go down. (Pinter, *Moonlight* 387)

By comparing Andy of *Moonlight* to Deeley of *Old Times*, Ghilardi demonstrated that the play attempts to reveal the usage of conversation as evasion. The effect of the past can never be eliminated, and its persistence is the effect of memory. The never-ending resonances of politics, religion and culture are deeply rooted in the human psyche. For example, the absence of women characters, or one may say the mere presence of female characters in Pinter's plays, opens up another challenging question for the patriarchal system. It also reveals that women (children, aged and marginalised) have no memory at all. They have no narrative, or one can consider it as their narratives being far from the mainstream ideology. One can see that the suppressed, marginalized, aged people, women and children are never considered seriously as the carriers of cultural memory.

The collective memories of the Holocaust and wars played a very important role in creating pauses, silences, oblivion and a kind of absurdity in life and art forms. Thinkers do believe that modern man is a by-product of war. He is not able to fess up to his own past deeds or have reasons to legitimise those beastly acts. So, he is in a rage like Andy in *Moonlight*, or could be in a half-awakened state, like Deborah in *A Kind of Alaska*. In both cases, the ownership of the past is in trouble. Whereas Deborah is constantly suspending the act of inheritance due to her illness, Andy is in anger due to the failure of inheritance.

The characters step back into the chaotic phase of human memory, which is full of ghostly appearances. They had no sense of truth and no wisdom at all. They were at a stage when there was nobody to carry forward the burden of the brutal acts. They share no sense of being inherited with humane and civil features. Life was more like a nightmare where mere ghosts, like Bridget, were walking around. The characters are awakened in somebody else's past, as Deborah is awakened by Hornby. Mark Batty suggested that:

> The fractured family structures in these two plays demonstrate the contradictory human impulses to either remain comfortably in a known situation or move on to new, self-enriching discoveries, and this contradiction played out within desired or regretfully fragmented family structures. Pinter has shown the family unit as a site for repression and social manipulation. He re-examined the site and explores the threats to its stability that it offers and regrets that are connected to it. (Batty 59)

4

Cultural Memory and Politics

Here they go again
The Yanks in their armored parade
Chanting their ballads of joy
As they gallop across the big world
Praising America's God
The gutters are clogged with the dead.

—Harold Pinter

Harold Pinter, with a strong impulse, defames the glorification of the War and its grand narrative. He has carried a sceptical attitude towards the war narratives. In post-war Europe, the reconstruction of the past took place through films, literature, paintings, memorials, museums and other art forms. Eventually, this process started generating profit for the State. The war narrative was full of different resonances and had become a powerful political tool. With the passage of time, the discourse of war became a collective story of the people. The discourse was manipulated and moulded according to the needs of the State. The purpose of the reconstruction of the war narratives was to channelise the traumatic moments and document history for the future. A direction and a political shape to the events were given by the very act of remembrance of those events. Revival of selective cultural memories became a collective-cultural-national practice in Europe. The present chapter undertakes a palimpsest research into the European war memories. Pinter makes an eclectic foray into the war narratives and unravels the memory games that the State was playing with the masses. Through his characters, Pinter projects how the war memories had become tools for political advantages. The memory that incorporates personal nuances is always framed through social parameters. It can be the most powerful medium to make or mar a generation.

Culture is a learned behaviour adapted through social and environmental conditions. It falls or arises on behalf of its enculturation methods (Rodriguez and Fortier 108). Culture is a truth and also a manner in which people understand their realities and construct their values with a correct meaning. Cultural memory is transcendental in nature. It means it remains embedded in people's psyche and is beyond the reach of everyday experiences. Cultures never exist in pure forms, so does the cultural memory of the people. At the core, any culture and its memory are so strong that they contain values and truth with the wisdom of past events. But at the periphery, it is equally flexible so that novel ideas or experiences are always welcomed through gossip or other communication tools. After the wars, the national rituals played a very important role in the identity formation of the various social groups. The rituals contained the personal, social and collective memories of the people in one act of remembrance. In Israel, Yom HaShoah comes a week before Independence Day. It is intentionally performed to remind people of the catastrophe of the Jewish Holocaust. It connects the birth of Israel on January 27 to the day when Auschwitz was attacked by the Red Army. One can consider this commemorative mourning act as an important part of memory culture that supports the embedded nostalgia (Winter 31). The State presented the war as a noble act. It was offered to the sacred land and to its people for future benefits. The official gatherings were being performed publicly in the form of rituals. No doubt, the people had different versions of the past and different opinions about it. In this context, the power of cultural memory appears in the form of religious performances that gather the people. The people choose particular memories and give those memories preference in the collective remembrance. The people who performed the remembrance acts themselves became memory activists. When one group of people ceases to transmit past experiences to the next generation, the tradition fails. As a result, someone else or other groups occupy their space and perform acts of remembrance.

The collective narratives had to combat the experiences of the past for supremacy. The contest finalised the design of the social group and the civic character of its people. Those in power always tried to construct and endorse their narrative in the market. Through marketing, they circulated and legitimised their deeds, including the wars too. In actuality, the market, which is the economic factor, is also governed and designed by the power. The socially, economically and politically dominant groups in a society always choose a particular set of memories, values and the whole lived experiences of the past for future benefits. That social group creates a supermarket for the set and sells it. The group wants to make the memory believable for the new generation.

The personal and collective narratives were manufactured at the same time during the act of war remembrance. The act of remembrance emerged with a new commercial aspect after the wars. The commoditisation of collective remembrance happened in Europe in the form of war memorials and mourning acts. Economic factors became the root cause of the commoditisation of the remembrance act. Both the expansion of trade and leisure time nourished the cultural memory acts and moulded the past memories according to its need in the present time (either of the golden past before urbanisation or the traumatic past of the wars and the Holocaust).

After the World Wars and the threatening Holocaust, the relationship between memory and mourning had become purely economic. Cultural memory is not all about the calculations of past catastrophes. It is made up of the multiple narratives of the indigenous, their values, beliefs, martyrs, leaders and heroes. All the facts are essential to build up a discourse for future generations. The various aspects of cultural memory are revered by that social group. They are then remembered in the memory of that particular group. Such acts of remembrance are then endorsed through celebrations, including religious ones.

Cultural memory is transmitted traditionally by its people, preserved in their narratives and dedicated to them. The merry-making celebration and sacred religious acts are not as simple as they seem. They are full of social and political pulls that gather the people with their consent. The people enjoin the sacred acts, enjoy them and, at the same time, feel divine experiences. These acts appear natural and soothing to people and are tuned in with their emotional cores. They heal their psychic wounds to some extent. People feel mesmerised and more alive during a celebration than before. These acts actually regenerate them. Steven Luke, an anthropologist, suggests that:

> The rituals are rule-governed activities of a symbolic character, which draw the attention of its participants to objects of thought and feeling which they consider to be of special significance. The rituals are not merely expressive acts. In fact formalized acts tend to be stylized, stereotyped and repetitive in nature. They always have religious connotations for their natives. The exotic rituals could be a mere lip-service or empty structure for the indigenous. (qtd. in Connerton 44)

The war memories shaped the national memory, history and the collective memory of the people in Europe. It had become a shared property of the people and the State. The State was indulged in the growth of the trades, and the war memories proved more sellable. The world around was ignorant about the tragedies of the war. So, Europe took advantage and presented the war as a sacred act that was offered to its people. Europe had created a market for it and targeted consumers worldwide. The world had looked upon the war as a unique experience. The State sold it to them as a noble act and a sacrificial offering to its people. The war memories were well paid for in a big consumer market. Their consumption was hyped in the international arena. They were cultivated through films, books, articles, photographs and media. The war history was sold in the form of biographies and autobiographies. One can see that the connection between memories had been commercialised in the act of mourning and by the objects of mourning, like offering flowers to the dead (souvenirs, photographs, letters, memoirs and, particularly, war cinema). Through mourning acts, they were paying mere lip service to the State.

Repeating the past and remembering it for some reasons are totally different acts. The collective acts of mourning conveyed a message of the loss of life and redemption. It created a false hope for a better world—where there would be more stability, prosperity and morality. The sentimental objects had their hidden motif and could easily touch the emotional core of people. No doubt, people suffered from multiple traumas. Still, they wanted to repeat what had happened to them in the past. Museums, films, arts, literature and memorials were the proof of it; they were the spaces where memory and imagery were bridged. The war memory contains both the history and the mystery of the wars. The cultural memory constitutes a national memory–making process; Eley's "popular memory," Youngblood's "authentic memory" and Bodnar's "collective memory" were all framed together under one national context (Winter 188). The popular memory constituted the cultural trends of that particular time. The authentic memory carried the wisdom of past events and validated the deeds of the past in the present. The collective memory was a social group's shared pool of experiences. Museums, films and art forms appealed to all kinds of memory claims. Taken together, social, literary and political embodiments were framed under one national brand in European culture. People started looking at wars as the sacrifices of soldiers for a nation rather than as a tragic experience. People visited cemeteries and battlefields. It had become a redemptive act at the collective level.

A Holocaust memorial was built near Brandenburg Gate in Berlin, the heart of the capital, to allure people. It was the symbol of identity formation for the Europeans. It focused on the national and political framework, which was damaged by the Nazis. The German government had debased it during the wars. Its construction was considered a metaphorical rebirth of the German nation or identity. The newly born economic culture had unique political and moral frames. Its aim was the stabilisation of identity as a commodity. But the Holocaust memories refused to inherit the traumatic past and any kind of stabilisation. The people repeated the past mechanically. It could not be considered as a traditional act of remembering.

The collective memory had the power to challenge national history. Winter suggests that in both the cases of history and memory, the basic question was how the World Wars and the Holocaust should be represented. The understanding of the past with historical facts has become a social phenomenon. Historical remembrance is actually the negotiation of the space between social memory and national history. "The public history is actually publicly funded history in the forms of museums and exhibitions" (Winter 38). The basic human right to talk about what had happened in the past or the traumatic experiences of the past had been invaded. The collective history and its various aspects had become significant in this case because an individual alone cannot create history. Public history had been stuck between social memory and national history.

History became a popular and money-making profession. Without any personal narrative, the construction of a national-social-political story was impossible. War experiences placed the family history in the universal context in the form of war memorials in Europe. The collective acts of remembrance connected the generations by sharing the tales of the same past. Many bestseller novels were about the war and war victims' families. The grandparents and grandchildren together visited past memories through films and museums. It is the best anecdote in which memory and history travel from one time-space to the next through a fictional landscape. It is the people, a society or a culture that carries the memory. Films, museums and other art forms also help evoke the memories of the past for people who lived through it and also for those who wanted to know about it. The people revisited the war memorials because they wanted to know what kind of people carried out that brutal act. They started looking at wars as the sacrifices of soldiers for the nation rather than as a tragic experience. People's revisits to the cemeteries and battlefields can be counted as a redemptive act at a collective level. One can consider it as a new collective and social language of mourning, which will lead to the secular world in the future.

War memory included three basic processes—construction, adaptation and circulation. Construction of memory was framed by arts, legal studies, science, academy and independent professions (Connerton 20). The construction of war memory emerged along with a cultural aspect that became a social memory. The personal memory of the people helped them gather social groups and recall the past. It provided the groups a unity and shape. In public spheres, people compliment, comment, discuss and criticise the past or whole lived experience. They also carry with them the images, gestures, expressions and the whole theatre of memory. They construct, transform, adapt and circulate war memory from personal to social to the national level.

War experience became a cultural myth for a new social and political system, in which ethnic identities emerged as the by-products of the World Wars and the Holocaust. One can analyse how the narratives of the State compete with the regional narratives in the twenty-first century memory cult in Europe. For instance, in the very name "Jewish-American Museum," the hyphen reveals the maintenance of ethnic identities in today's world, which is possible only through cultural memory. The cultural memory provides the space as well as the resistance to its people. The museum is a bridge between the Jews and the Americans. The hyphen identities become more powerful, adaptable and circulate through national commemorative acts. The most crucial aspect of war memory was that every narrative of the past became a national memory or collective memory. It could be understood as a shared property of the citizens and the State (Winter 117). The people manufactured their civic character for future generations with the aid of cultural memory. The most important factor in cultural memory was how people looked at themselves as a nation. The people revisited the past and honoured it on the State's behalf. The State used the people who then perceived the past as a prism in order to view the new conflicts of the future.

The turning points in the history of Europe were the periods of industrialisation, wars and the Holocaust. Cultural memory was constructed through historical narratives that were written, published, recited in schools and performed in public places. The cultural memory formed through these upheavals is preserved through texts, narratives, rites and monuments. Connerton, the eminent social memory thinker, wrote in *How Societies Remember*:

> War memories pervaded all the spheres of life, the festivals of the Reich being related to the feast of the Christian calendar...the seizure of power in January 1933 and the outbreak of war in 1939, the subjects of Third Reich were constantly reminded of the National Socialist Party...and the liturgical year began on 30th January with the anniversary of Hitler's seizure of power in 1933. (Connerton 41)

Living in the memory-filled world depended upon the lash income sources and leisure time. Fortunately, both were in abundance for Europeans after industrialisation. Machines had replaced man and were more efficient than man. The acts of memorisation changed identity into a mere commodity that could be consumed by everyone. To have a common identity meant that one shared a common narrative of the past. It created a homogenous mass. The marketing of memory was well paid in the world market in the form of films, books, articles, photographs and television. The gossip that is an innate part of culture also had a strong foothold in the formation of the homogenous mass. It was so important for culture because it touched the core of its people and also transmuted individual experiences. During the war, social (gossip) and political (news and statements) aspects merged. There was no demarcation between them.

In Pinter's plays, one cannot judge whether the characters are merely communicating or shooting political remarks at each other. Pinter's plays are full of political resonances. The gossip and under-toned political comments of the characters have become a genuine formula for breeding political hegemony in European culture. In Pinter's plays, it seems as if the State speaks through the innocent people's minds. But at the same time, Pinter also makes the people's voices resonate with what the State wants them to echo. Pinter astonishingly dramatises it on the stage through his characters. The formation of a common identity means sharing almost a common set of narratives about the past with the social group. The British National Trust targeted the nostalgia of war-stricken people and played cultural politics in Europe. No doubt the economic factors were behind the facade but the political strategies were more powerful. Earnest Renan considered the memory (especially the disrupted memories created during urbanization and war) as "political glue" and pointed it out in his lecture (in Paris) in 1882, entitled *What Is a Nation?*, that:

> A nation is a soul, a spiritual principle. Two things which in truth, are carefully one, constitute this soul, this spiritual principle. One is the past, the other is the present. One is the possession in common, of a rich legacy of memories; the other is present day consent, the desire to live together, the will to continue to value the undivided heritage that one has received.... To have the glory of the past in common, a shared will in the present; to have done great deeds together, and want to do more of them, are the essential conditions for the constitution of a people.... One loves the house which one has built and passes on. (qtd. in Winter 24)

From an early age, Pinter was engaged in the politics of the world around him. When he was eighteen, he expressed disgust for the Cold War politics and The Labour Party's endorsement of the American nuclear presence in British culture. Pinter had become a member of an anti-apartheid organisation. He was agitated over what he saw in Vietnam and South Africa. Pinter, with his friend Arthur Miller, visited Turkey. They publicly condemned the human rights abuse that they had witnessed there. He attended an anti-Thatcher discussion group and wrote numerous public condemnations of American and British foreign policy since the end of World War II. His Nobel Prize acceptance speech, *Art, Truth and Politics*, is a masterpiece. Mel Gussow, in 1993, asked Pinter whether he would ever write about the Holocaust. Pinter replied, "I don't know. There's something in me that wants to do something about it. It's so difficult" (qtd. in Billington 385). Pinter finally broached that subject in 1996 when he wrote *Ashes to Ashes*.

While writing the opening lines of *Ashes to Ashes*, Pinter reminisces about the Nazi atrocities. The play becomes more influential with its structural significance. Its structure reveals the distorted memory and temporal disturbance within the play. The structural and thematic arrangement in the play provides the audience with some way of articulating what one can already sense. The play *Ashes to Ashes* emerged from Pinter's reading of Gitta Sereny's biography of Albert Speer (a German architect with Nazis during WWII) while on holiday. Pinter had been struck by the image of Speer visiting the slave labour factories, for which he himself was responsible. Pinter added that reading the book had channelised a number of his own associations with the past. He had always been haunted by the image of the Nazis picking up babies on bayonet spikes and throwing them out of the window.

Pinter based the love story in *Ashes to Ashes* on Sereny's Postscript, which recounts Speer's love affair towards the end of his life. He was by then in his mid-seventies, and the woman he loved was half his age. She had contacted Speer after reading his memoirs and found that it helped her understand her own past. Although Speer had described her as a young Englishwoman, she was, in fact, a German who had settled in England and was married, with two children, to an Englishman. If one tries to relate it to the play, one can see that a part of Rebecca's character has been derived from the anonymous young woman mentioned in Speer's biography. However, the character of Rebecca recounts the stories as if she had experienced them herself. It seemed as if she had accompanied her lover on his visits to the slave labour camps and the factories. Rebecca's fascination with her lover's sexual violence may be a way out for Pinter to showcase that unnamed young woman's attraction to one of the central figures of the Third Reich. When Mireia Aragay asked Pinter about Nazism in *Ashes to Ashes*, he answered:

> No, I don't think so at all. It is about the images of Nazi Germany; I don't think anyone can ever get out of their mind. Holocaust is probably the worst thing that ever happened because it was also calculated by the people who actually did it. Their view of it is very significant.

> They counted how many people they were murdering every day and they looked upon it, I take it, like a car delivery service. How many cars can you make in one day? How many people can you kill in one day? And there is the whole question of how many people knew what 'repressive, cynical and indifferent acts of murder, selling arms to brutal regimes... in *Ashes to Ashes* I'm not simply talking about Nazis. I'm talking about us, and our conception of our past and our history and what it does to us in the present. (qtd. in Billington 386)

Ashes to Ashes is a one-act play. The play is set in a time 'now' (the time 'now' has a symbolic meaning; it means the past is changed into mere ashes now). Early evening but no light outside and lamplight inside the living room intensify the situation in a room in a country house. One can see how a very elegant country room's window opens towards the corridors of European history. History was a crucial point in European culture for substantial changes and was preserved in cultural memory. Billington and others have pursued the offered lead that links the figure of the lover (Rebbeca's lover) with the Nazi leader Speer, a close associate of Hitler.

Both Devlin and Rebecca, in their forties, seem to be passionate lovers in the play. At first glance, one cannot judge their relationship. In fact, in the end, the mystery of their relationship remains. Rebecca's name/identity suggests she is Jewish, separating her inner world from her partner Devlin. Devlin, which is an Irish name/identity, is excluded from pure Jewish experiences. No doubt, the difference between their attitudes is gendered. One can also perceive a cultural divide between Jews and Gentiles. As the play grows, it becomes clear that they are husband and wife, although their relationship is not defined in the play. Initially, Devlin seems to be Rebecca's husband, lover or a brute interrogator who might kill her in the end. He compels her to answer each question. She reveals personal information throughout the play. Rebecca's opening lines may well be intended to taunt Devlin or suggest to him that a previous relationship still affects her in some way. The explanation for Rebecca's excursions into the past might have come from possible influences of Speer's biography of Pinter. In the first attempt, she narrates a tale of sexual abuse and fear of death. Devlin stands in a gesture of power, and Rebecca sits. It shows that she is under his control. She passively answers as if she has been hypnotised by Devlin. Whatever he interrogates in the play, she clarifies:

Rebecca: Well…for example…he would stand over me and clench his fist. And then he had put his other hand on my neck and grip it and bring my head towards him. His fist…grazed my mouth. And he'd say, 'kiss my fist.'

> Devlin: And did you?
>
> Rebecca: Oh, yes. I kissed his fist. The knuckles. And then he'd open his hand and give me the palm of his hand…to kiss…which I kissed. (*Pause*)
>
> And then I would speak. (Pinter, *Ashes to Ashes* 395)

The opening scene of the play is full of brutality. This claim of hers is, of course, structurally, thematically and visually reproduced and reinforced by Devlin's putting his hands around her throat (in precisely the same manner according to her account at the beginning of the play and, even more significantly, by the echo of her account at the end). Devlin might interpret Rebecca's account of her lover's hand around her throat as a clue for him to repeat the action, but the audience knows otherwise. It looks like the tale of a two-fold power structure. It is the enactment of domination on the one hand, but on the other, it is full of anxiety, insecurity and reckless curiosity. Rebecca's tales of the frozen moments that she may not have experienced personally bring one closer to those moments. One would not be certain whether the atrocities had actually occurred in her life. The living room window functions as a film screen, on which a silent movie is being projected, and Rebecca seems to enter the film she has been watching.

One can see an English country house where a jealous husband questions his wife about past relationships. Despite their physical presence, Rebecca and Devlin inhabit totally disparate inner worlds. The act of interrogation is performed almost smoothly without any disturbances. Sometimes it appears to be a well-knitted narrative of the Holocaust. The State is constructing a fine narrative of the past for the future through Devlin and Rebecca's characters in the play. The audience perceives exactly what the power wants to circulate about the past in the upcoming future. One can see the construction and the circulation of the war memories in *Ashes to Ashes*.

The multilayered discourse makes the experiences of the characters in the play more real than the mere narrative of the past. The verbal game is not played innocently in the play. The communication among the characters is full of political resonances behind the scenes. Words are empty barrels, but when one scrutinises them subtly, they would find them to be full of meaningful echoes. One of the most common pastimes among people is recalling past memories. Everyone believes that they remember the same things in the same order. But Pinter never allowed his characters to do this and, in fact, parodied the slow incremental progress in narration. It is conducted in such a way as to balance all inequalities through simple gossip. Whenever a character in his plays attempts to create a common past, another character knowingly disrupts the process, which could be considered manipulation. This is also applicable to past memories that are disturbing and plainly false. The disruption is often effected by calling the time frame itself into question. Thus, Rebecca intentionally describes how her lover used to hold her around the throat. Devlin suddenly shifts the time frame:

> Devlin: Do you feel you're being hypnotized?
>
> Rebecca: When?
>
> Devlin: Now?
>
> Rebecca: No. (Pinter, *Ashes to Ashes* 397)

Pinter's approach to time has been strongly influenced by Henri Bergson and his theories of duration. Bergson suggested, "The separation of memory into discrete units, which then appear discontinuous, is caused by certain lapses in our span of attention" (qtd. in Regal 4). By this process, says Bergson, one tends to falsely see certain individual events as representing stages in the development of our minds and, therefore, identify them as changes. Devlin's question about her being hypnotised is in the present time because he has used the present tense. But Rebecca is not sure whether he is referring to the present or the past. Throughout the play, it becomes more profound that Devlin knows less than Rebecca about the past. He demands the authentic details of the past with exact time and place, while her responses are made up of dream-like tales that clearly do not include him. The play has a kind of sexual brutality and submission to it through Rebecca. After this, Devlin asks her instantly, "Rebecca: I think you are a fuckpig" (Pinter, *Ashes to Ashes* 398). A similar disruption takes place a little further on when Devlin asks, absurdly whether the man she is speaking of had any eyes. Rebecca replies, "What colour?" (Pinter, *Ashes to Ashes* 400).

Rebecca's conscious shifts in time zones from past to present or present to past are intended to throw Devlin off balance. This technique is common enough in Pinter's memory plays but is especially utilised in the play *Ashes to Ashes*. Rebecca's various past tales and memories are more than a battle for personal gain and reveal the power structure in Europe. *Ashes to Ashes* is a haunting play with changing time zones. Pinter shows how the human mind is swinging in various time zones simultaneously and can easily be handled according to the need of time.

The play also reveals the male desire to possess the female's past, as seen in *Old Times*, the relation between interrogator and victim, as in *One For the Road*, and cruelty and barbarism, as in *Mountain Languages* and *Party Time*. In this play, real and unreal merge effortlessly. *Ashes to Ashes* is a play of minimum physical actions but maximum mental and verbal performances or memory spillovers. Devlin puts several questions to Rebecca about her lover's height, breadth and depth and suddenly starts addressing her as "darling:"

> Devlin: That's precisely the question I'm asking you… my darling.
>
> Rebecca: How odd to be called darling. No one has ever called me darling. Apart from my lover. (Pinter, *Ashes to Ashes* 400)

The shattered narrative of the people has reformed now, and the dialogues between Devlin and Rebecca are perfectly designed by Pinter to show this act of narration through remembrance. Rebecca recalls:

> Rebecca: I think it had something to do with a travel agency. I think he was some kind of courier. No. No, he wasn't. That was only a part-time job. I mean that was only part of the job in the agency. He was quite high up, you see. He had a lot of responsibilities. (Pinter, *Ashes to Ashes* 403)

Rebecca's abstract answers raise suspicion about her stance. She exhibits reluctance in providing straight and definite answers. Her past seems more authentic than her present when she describes how her ex-lover took her to the factory. Devlin investigates in detail, and she reveals the depths during the course of the play. She even has the capability to transport Devlin to the past world and creates a cadence reciting:

> Rebecca: They were all wearing caps...the workpeople... soft caps...and they took them off when he came in, leading me, when he led me down the alleys between the rows of workpeople. (Pinter, *Ashes to Ashes* 405)

Further, she explained they had total faith in him (her lover). They respected his purity and conviction. They would follow him in the future for authenticity. Devlin had become the benchmark for the truth of the past. Rebecca's changing statements about her lover or past intensify the tension between the characters in the play. In the beginning, she said that he was the head of a factory and then a worker for a travel agency. Later on, she suddenly revealed that he was a guide. She says:

> Rebecca: He was a guide. He used to go to the local railway station and walk down the platform and tear all the babies from the arms of their screaming mothers. (Pinter, *Ashes to Ashes* 406)

Her difficulty in deciding on the job seems puzzling. When forced by Devlin to provide the information about the travel agency, she states that her lover was a guide, as though this would explain it all. Devlin then asks her, "Was he a tourist guide?"

(Pinter, *Ashes to Ashes* 407). This question she leaves unanswered. Here, Pinter is showing a kind of sexual repression that was an innate part of fascism from the very beginning. Fascism later achieved an extremity showcasing a brutal enactment of power and naked submission to it. Rebecca can also be perceived as a symbol of vulnerability, including femininity and gendered memory. She represents innocent people who are the culprits in the very hands of the State or patriarchy, which is represented by Devlin. This play not only depicts the Nazis' picture but also the distorted memories of the common folk. Rebecca explains the atrocities in the following words:

> Rebecca: I wanted to go to the bathroom. But I simply couldn't find it. I looked everywhere. I'm sure they had one. But I never found out where it was. (Pinter, *Ashes to Ashes* 406)

Like other plays of Pinter, this play too features a man and a woman who present conflicting views, experiences and memories. Pinter sets these characters against one another. His female characters are more poetic and lyrical in expression, especially Rebecca in *Ashes to Ashes*. Devlin has the authority to formulate time, and Rebecca inhabits in that time.

Memory, too, is gendered to some extent because women have no language, narrative and no right to access memory. They are trained to remember what active, powerful and patriarchic counterparts want them to remember. In any culture, the adherence to stories, whether real or unreal, is very fruitful for its future. The narrative has entered into scholarship through literature, school and a movement on the academic left, which is affiliated with feminism and critical race theory (Hinchman and Hinchman 3). Women, children and old people, including the marginalised, all belong to the same group. They can easily be manipulated by the power structures. The civilisation's highest achievements seem like mere superstructures designed to maintain powerful groups' meaningful history. Rebecca seems accustomed to such an authority. Rebecca tries to change the subject of inquiry by talking about the echoing sounds of police sirens. She hears the police siren but is upset when it fades away. She utters:

> Rebecca: I'm just terribly upset...as the siren fades away in my ears I knew it was becoming louder and louder for somebody else...
>
> Devlin: Don't worry, there'll always be another one. There's one in its way to you now. Believe me. You'll hear it again soon. Any minute. (Pinter, *Ashes to Ashes* 408)

In some cases, it seems, time does not heal. In fact, it cuts even deeper wounds. It is only while the police siren is sounding that Rebecca feels comfortable. She feels insecure without it and asserts:

> Rebecca: I hate it fading away. I hate it echoing away. I hate it leaving me. I hate losing it. I hate somebody else possessing it. I want it to be mine, all the time. It's such a beautiful sound. Don't you think? (Pinter, *Ashes to Ashes* 408).

When danger is clearly announced, Rebecca has a share in the present moment. When the alarm fades or echoes away, she knows that the foothold has gone. When Rebecca explains to Devlin how a "perfectly innocent pen" rolled off the coffee table, Devlin warns her that she can't say things like the pen is innocent. He is reconstructing reality through words and playing a power game by controlling or twisting it.

> Rebecca: This pen, this perfectly innocent pen . . .
>
> Devlin: . . . You don't know how many other hands have held it, how many other hands have written with it, what other people have been doing with it. You know nothing of its history. You know nothing of its parents' history. (Pinter, *Ashes to Ashes* 410)

Devlin's linguistic twists also become a part of power play rather than a mere verbal game. He distorts and recreates the past according to his need in the present. But he himself feels insecure in a quicksand situation while interrogating her. He lives in a world that is full of terror and exists without God. He claims:

> Devlin: God is sinking into a quicksand... It will be like England playing Brazil at Wembley and not a soul in the stadium. Can you imagine? Playing both halves to a

> totally empty house… A world without a winner. (Pinter, *Ashes to Ashes* 412)

Another Pinter's character in *One for the Road*, named Nicolas, claims that maybe God was speaking through him. And he himself felt threatened and imagined a world without God. The characters of Pinter belong to a society without faith, God and goodness where there would only be victims and victimizers and both losers. Devlin also represents power and, at the same time, feels powerless. He wants to possess Rebecca's body, soul, past, present and future, but he himself feels like a victim of the same power who disempowers Rebecca.

Pinter wrote about atrocities and human suffering. The newspapers reported these atrocities every day. The characters embody the essence of the title, *Ashes to Ashes*. But the "ashes" in this play have a narrower denotation—it signifies the ashes of the Jews cremated in the death camps. All that remains of these people are memories, and Rebecca's memories evoke her own Holocaust memories.

Rebecca yields to her lover's brutal handling, to his use of force, becoming a willing victim. The gap between the two characters is also attributable to the gendered characterisation of the war memories. One belongs to the sensitive woman, and the other to her insensitive partner. Pinter is interested in the internal, rather than the external, reality. The two different realities are juxtaposed in Rebecca's recollection of what she saw one day through the garden window in Dorset. Through a monologue, she describes how she stood by the window on a sunny summer day in Dorset. She watched a crowd of people who seemed very cold and wore coats. They were walking towards the sea and into the water. To pick up the main motif of the play, Pinter mentions twice the guides that ushered the people across the beach through Rebecca's character. Pinter creates a frame in which the window of the English house, looking southward towards the sea and the continent, opens onto a nightmare vision of the Holocaust. The people walk into the sea carrying all their bags, like the children of Israel, into the Red Sea, except that no miracle occurs, and they are drowned. Thus, one neither needs to know how these characters arrived nor where they might be going after the action is over. Rebecca is using her memory in a battle of wits with Devlin. One must know how and why she is doing it, even if one does not. Like Devlin, one will almost certainly wonder about the authority that gives him the right to inquire. He questions Rebecca:

> Devlin: What authority do you think you yourself possess which would give you the right to discuss such an atrocity?
>
> Rebecca: I have no such authority. Nothing has ever happened to me. Nothing has ever happened to any of my friends. I have never suffered. Nor have my friends.
> Devlin: Good...it's not just your head in his hands... it's your life...your spiritual...welfare. (Pinter, *Ashes to Ashes* 413)

Throughout the play, she is forced to remember what she might have never seen or what had happened before she was even born. In the above disclaimer, she seems to distance herself from any direct contact with the Holocaust experiences she herself describes. Despite the fact that she could not have possibly experienced the atrocities herself, Rebecca's disturbing memories are nonetheless authentic. Clearly, what she has read and heard from survivors' reports has become part of her own consciousness.

The play answers the questions related to the revocation of war memories in a culture. It also showcases the process of their construction and adaptation through Rebecca's character. There is always a little doubt if she is authentically reliving a memory or whether it is her own. The void between Rebecca's recollection of the Nazi atrocities and the everyday calm of her English surroundings creates an ambiguity. Rebecca remembers the atrocities and is now in her forties in 1996, as the play is set in the time 'Now.' Thus, in fact, she must have been too young to have witnessed them or might not have been born at that time. She can also represent the modern generation that is not allowed to forget the cultural memory. She has to relive the pain and is forced to remember the anguish of the victims. Her memories resonate in the audience's own consciousness, evoking the memory of the Holocaust.

Pinter's well-known interest in the role of memory in consciousness intersects the contemporary preoccupation with the question of recording survivors' testimonials (Scolnicov 1). Rebecca's insistence on being alone in the house emphasises the loneliness of her experience (being a Jew) and her sense of being a stranger. She perceives things differently from the mainstream. Being a Jew himself, Pinter knows how the inner perception of the *Shoah* ("calamity" in Hebrew) or the Holocaust distinguishes Jews from the society that surrounds him. Rebecca and Devlin may share an English house, but Devlin has no share in Rebecca's inner world. In Pinter's plays, this inner world is of greater significance than the external reality. It is made up of Rebecca's memories.

As a sensitive person, Rebecca identifies with the suffering, in contrast to Devlin, who shows insensitivity to it. Being a representative of women, marginal and Jews, she refuses Devlin's presence in such experiences. He was not part of her personal memory at that turning point in European history. That is why she specifically excludes him from her account of her Dorset experience by insisting that he was not there:

> Rebecca: Oh no, you weren't there. I don't think anyone else was there. No, I was all by myself. I was alone... And I saw all these people walk into the sea. The tide covered them slowly. Their bags bobbed about in the waves. (Pinter, *Ashes to Ashes* 416)

Devlin is not a part of her account, as he represents the State. He is the victimiser who cannot understand the plight of the victim. Through Rebecca's dialogue, one can see how the State-power manipulates the past traumatic memories of the individuals. The State has the power to make or mar individual and personal memories in this way. One may see how the State apparatus failed during World War II and the Holocaust. Rebecca's description of a crowd of people drowned in a sea is a direct reference to the atrocities of the Holocaust. The reference to the crowd drowning in a sea echoes the sense of oppression in her lover's factory or English society. She herself is a victim of this oppressed society and a figment of mental elephantiasis in her own words, and she blames Devlin, saying:

> Rebecca: The mental elephantiasis means that when you spill an ounce of gravy becomes a vast sea of gravy... You brought it on yourself. You are not the victim of it, you are the cause of it. It was you who handed over the bundle. (Pinter, *Ashes to Ashes* 417)

One can see Rebecca's deliberate entry into someone else's memory. Certain events occur in human history that are indelibly sketched into the minds of not only those who have witnessed them but all who have heard about them. They become an inseparable part of one's consciousness in a real and actual sense. Rebecca, in remembering someone else's past, illustrates that certain atrocities haunt all our minds and that she needs no authority to be the mouthpiece of the present moment. Part of the pain she is clearly suffering from results from not being able to reconcile with her former lover's attention. In this sense, whether or not she personally experienced the horror of having her baby torn from her arms is less significant than the fact that some women have actually gone through this terrible experience. She becomes the representative of such mothers, and her remembrance of the event makes the snatching occur again. Rebecca lives in a half-real world between dream and reality. Like other memory plays, it also revolves around past echoes, dreams, memories and illusions—a kind of mental life or inner life that Pinter could capture exactly as it occurred there. Both the characters oscillate between real and unreal worlds—Devlin shifts her to a harsh reality of real life for more control over Rebecca and the situation too. Devlin says:

> Devlin: Now look, let's start again. We live here. You don't live in Dorset... or anywhere else. You live here with me. This is our house. You have a nice sister. She lives close to you. She has two lovely kids. You are their aunt. You like that...

> Rebecca: I don't think we can start again. We started...a long time ago. We started. We can't start again. We can't end again. (Pinter, *Ashes to Ashes* 424)

When Rebecca claims that she and Devlin can end "again and again and again" (Pinter, *Ashes to Ashes* 425), she may be referring not only to their relationship but to something much more profound. It is she who starts singing after a long interrogation throughout the play. Music or song is an important cultural activity and full of the act of remembrance. Music nourishes the people and has a perfect narrative order. Humans, when born, listen to lullabies and want to lie in cadenced graves. Stephen Crites reveals that music can be a survival sign for people. It defines the manners of the people and relates them to the world around them. Crites claims that:

> The narrative, like music, is a cultural form reflecting our existence as temporal creatures. Experience...is already an incipient story made coherent by memory. While, we live forward we understand backwards. Memory, through which we perceive events in a simple before-and-after sequence, gives rise to recollection involving the artful, though by no means arbitrary, transformation, of mere chronological sequence into full-blown narratives. (Hinchman and Hinchman 3)

The tune Rebecca and Devlin sing during the course of the play resonates with its title and supports the issue of the play that every time, death is remembered. It brings a new ending.

In the end, Rebecca finds herself in a room of a tall building where she sees an old man and a little boy who are dragging suitcases. In Rebecca's vision of the people heading for the water, Pinter has captured the haunting image of the ordered walking into the sea as well as the intense cold. In her second vision through a window, towards the end of the play, Rebecca goes a step further in her identification with the victims of the Holocaust. She sees an old man and a little boy walking down the street, dragging big suitcases, on an icy, star-lit night. Then, she notices a woman following them, carrying a baby in her arms. The woman kissed the baby, a girl, then listened to its heartbeat and breathing. Suddenly, watching the woman through the window of her English home, Rebecca entered the scene, assuming the role of the mother, completely turning herself into a Holocaust victim.

Rebecca's dazzling surrealist Holocaust visions through the window demonstrate that, for her, the accounts of the atrocities have become profound memories. These cultural memories cannot be put aside and laid to rest. In *Ashes to Ashes*, Pinter shows that, for us too, they have become profound memories and that we too can never lay them to rest: "I'm talking about us and our conception of our past and our history, and what it does to us in the present" (qtd. in Billington 385). Rebecca sings "Ashes to ashes," and Devlin carries on the song, singing "And dust to dust" (Pinter, *Ashes to Ashes* 425). She recalls in the last part of the play the exact cultural representation of Nazi soldiers selecting women and children at the railway stations to transport them to concentration camps. She begins narrating the tale in the third person:

> Rebecca: Anyway, I was about to close the curtains but then I suddenly saw a woman following them, carrying a baby in her arms... She stood still. She kissed her baby. The baby was a girl...the baby was breathing. (Pinter, *Ashes to Ashes* 427)

Pinter, through his play, brought genocide to British shores through doubtful memories of Rebecca and raised many questions about the authenticity of those memories. She has become that woman in a dream who has experienced the past. One is not sure about the characters and their situations. Maybe she herself was that woman, and Rebecca's lover was Devlin himself, who wanted to change the brutal acts of the past for his personal benefit. In the end, Rebecca imaginatively meets the victim woman at the station:

> Rebecca: They took us to the trains
> Echo: The trains
> [...]
> Rebecca: They were taking the babies away
> Echo: The babies away

Rebecca: I took my baby and wrapped it in my shawl
Echo: My shawl
Rebecca: And I made it into a bundle
Echo: A bundle
Rebecca: And I held it under my left arm
Echo: My left arm
Pause.
Rebecca: And I went through with my baby
Echo: My baby
Pause.
Rebecca: But the baby cried out
Echo: Cried out
Rebecca: And the man called me back.
Echo: Called me back
Rebecca: And he said what do you have there?
Echo: Have there?
Rebecca: He stretched out his hand for the bundle
Echo: For the bundle
Rebecca: And I gave him the bundle
Echo: The bundle
Rebecca: And that's the last time I held the bundle
Echo: The bundle
Silence.
Rebecca: And we got on the train
Echo: The train
Rebecca: And we arrived at this place
Echo: This place
Rebecca: And I met a woman I knew... (Pinter, *Ashes to Ashes* 430)

Although the Holocaust and the Nazis are never mentioned in the play, the images evoked—the railway platform, the babies snatched from their crying mothers' arms, the winter scenes and the strange factory—all imagery point toward that way. Holocaust imagery has become an important part of their day-to-day lives and appears in conversations. The war trauma has lingered in the survivor's minds. Bodnar's vision about the war traumas strengthens the theme of the play, and Rebecca's role in the play emphasizes the situation of being a victim and a victimizer. She twists the situation and, at the same time, feels manipulated by Devlin too. Bodnar said that:

> The traumas of war were not buried but displaced in cinema and cinematic techniques in other arts like literature-overlapping of memory and imagery collaborations. It was direct psychopathology in cultural productions. The word "trauma" has defined the whole culture at that time. (qtd. in Winter 192)

The concluding monologue of Rebecca in the play ties together different strands of Holocaust memories—the train, the mother, the bundle and the snatching of the babies. In her final words, Rebecca identifies herself completely with the image of the mother whose baby has been snatched from her hands and murdered. At one point, she even undergoes the heart-wrenching denial of ever having had a baby. Having imaginatively stepped into Holocaust memory, Rebecca completely refuses to cooperate with Devlin. Martin S. Regal sees *Ashes to Ashes* as a lyrical play rather than dramatic work as it demands extreme audience concentration. The play hardly presents itself as a piece of reality. Rebecca becomes more lyrical and rhythmical in the last part. She muses:

> Rebecca: And she said what happened to your baby.
> Echo: your baby
> Rebecca: where is your baby?
> Echo: your baby
> Rebecca: and I said your baby
> Echo: what baby
> Rebecca: I don't have a baby
> Echo: a baby
> Rebecca: I don't know of any baby
> Echo: of any baby
> Rebecca: I don't know of any baby...of any baby...,
> Long silence. Blackout. (Pinter, *Ashes to Ashes* 432)

The symbolic state or territory represented by Rebecca in the play has now become childless and has no future. Pinter has successfully designed a personal dialogue with political resonances throughout the play. The play reveals the act of memory formation and its adaptation in the present time through Rebecca and Devlin's characters. Devlin constructs the memory through Rebecca, and she adapts it culturally.

A culture that exhibits no memory means it has no history, and having no history signifies that it never existed. It is thus customary in any culture to memorize. Through memorization, one is able to recognize his identity. In post-war Europe, the State aimed at erasing some events and reconstructing particular memories that could eventually generate a history of its own. Primarily, memory could be conceptualised through socialisation. Pinter's well-known biographer Mark Batty considered memory a very sensitive tool for achieving political advantages. He termed Pinter as a playwright who dealt with memory types. He comments:

> Our actual memories are very easily manipulated, distorted and changed, so that we don't remember what had exactly occurred in the past. Pinter was agitated over the growing gulf between the lived experience and its distorted representation through language which is the most powerful weapon for politicians in democratic world. The State was cultivating brainwashed human photocopies. The State hegemony curtailed the thought process of the automatons. Pinter said, "That's what they're doing, they're dropping the Atom Bomb to keep the world clean for democracy." (Batty 77)

Analysis of cultural memory is a significant step to study the traces of actual traumatic events that have shaped European history. After the traumas of War and the Holocaust, people lost the capability to think. So they were overridden by the power. For Pinter, it was necessary to dig out the traces and keep them as authentic records of the past. In his plays, Pinter presents skulls and skeletons rather than human minds and bodies on the stage (dinner tables in *Celebration*), which resonates with memories. The mind can think, rethink and speak. But the skulls cannot do so. They are carrying mere traces of the past for echoing in the future. He admitted that the play *Celebration* was actually drawn from his own memories of European culture. The European culture had been transformed into a culture of mere celebrations without any content. The war memories had been constructed according to the needs of the present times, adapted by the people, circulated and sold to the world around. The State had earned enough money because World Wars proved to be a profitable trade for the Europeans. In fact, the State earned a lot of wealth, fame and sympathy from the world. A political game had been played out by the State. Now it was the time to celebrate the resurrection of Europe. The State believed that one should carry the golden past (State's golden history) and recall it during merry-making acts. The valour and glory should be shared with the next generation, and in the process, the ideology of prosperity should be transmitted. In this way, Europeans could heal the war traumas and create a successful narrative order for the future.

Pinter could perceive the façade and considered it as an idiom of lies. Through his art, he projected people's mentality that was being stuffed with merry-making social acts. The past tragedy was being paid mere lip service. The celebrants in his play were seen celebrating rather than mourning over and over again. Pinter projected meaninglessness that existed both on the surface and at the bottom of society. The act of celebration gathers the people to make them feel they are one. It raises their faith in pedigree, purity of blood and communal sense of living. But through his absurd drama, Pinter revealed how the characters were cheating upon each other as well as the audience. The celebrations were designed for political advantages. The play *Celebration* opens up with a new perspective of celebrations.

The play's title *Celebration* is ironic as one can see that it appeals, on the one hand, to desperation and to celebration on the other. Pinter points out that one should not cry over the tragic past or the meaninglessness of given life. So, if one need not mourn the past trauma, one must enjoy it and, while celebrating, mock it. Pinter projected how memory could be suppressed if it was uncomfortable, painful and not suitable for negotiation. Pinter once said:

> One has to know what happened and face it and I think everybody has to do that. I think our actual memories are very easily manipulated, distorted and changed, so that we don't remember. There's so much that happens in the media and through the structures of the way we live, that half of the time we don't know what we're actually being suspected to. (qtd. in Batty 75)

The Holocaust has been a turning point in European history. It directs people towards more meaninglessness of human life and challenges human knowledge too. It was a giant black hole in the midst of our Universe of Reason (Winter 31). In *Celebration*, one can see the characters' efforts to come out of the void. They want to fill the abyss through various superfluous indulgences. They were occupying themselves with celebrations, residing in a fantasy world full of treasures and a number of sexual encounters. By hook or crook, the characters were trying to find a solution to their hollowness. No doubt they failed to find a reasonable answer for living their lives. But, constantly, they are pretending to be happy and satisfied by indulging in each and every trend offered by the new millennium. Both the sense of being guilty or of being over clever simmers throughout the play. To some extent, they behave as neurotics, a bit obsessed and are unable to carry the guilt of the past on their shoulders. So, with every changing moment, they change the subjects and start over again and again, tasting the rich and delicious lives. Pinter's audience was not scrutinizing the actual lives of the celebrants while enjoying the play or sharing the experiences of oneness with the diners on the stage. Pinter succeeded in creating oneness on the stage. But the play in itself examined the empty lives of the celebrant characters. It did so with a combination of fury, humor, compassion and hope that one could indeed celebrate after a cultural trauma. *Celebration* was a cautionary play for the new era. Katherine H. Burkman wrote in *Desperation in Harold Pinter's Celebration* that the play had a kind of double irony. It was a play about desperation and focused on celebrations (Burkman 1).

The play is full of loneliness and desperation. The characters seem nostalgic about something better in the memories of the golden past. The plot revolves around three couples dining in the most expensive restaurant in London (an allusion to the Ivy restaurant of London). The restaurant setting in itself is a metaphor for fragile happiness and harmony in society. The play starts with the Waiter's words:

> Waiter: Who's having the duck?
>
> Lambert: The duck's for me.
>
> Julie: No it isn't. (Pinter, *Celebration* 3)

The waiter's pretentious ignorance is suggested by the opening lines of the play. Throughout the play, it is difficult for the audience to find whether the waiter is innocent or cleverer than the diners. The question arises that if the place is a lavish restaurant in the city, how can the interruptions of a mere waiter interrupt the whole ambience of the elitist culture? In the play, the waiter could be the symbol of a marginal's memory that comes and goes. The mainstream diners provide just a lane for such a narrative but never consider it seriously.

In the beginning, there are only two couples on the stage, Lambert and Julie and Matt and Prue. They are celebrating Lambert and Julie's wedding anniversary. The men are brothers who are married to two sisters. Lambert, however, has to be reminded that it is his anniversary. The order of duck, it seems, is for Julie, who doesn't care about the order. Lambert's lack of knowledge and childlike demands strike the tone of desperation in the play. It underlies his behaviour throughout the play. He insists that:

> Lambert: And for me. I mean what about me? What did I order? I haven't the faintest idea? What did I order? (Pinter, *Celebration* 4)

When Prue tells him he has ordered Osso Buco, he has no idea what it is. The exaggerated discussion of the food items directs the audience to loveless marriages and the general anguish suffered by the couples. What keeps them together, other than a general vacuity, anger and emptiness, is a link with the past memories. It is their ignorance about the past that they have never experienced themselves. The waiter knowingly interjects throughout the play. He is the only connecting link who tries to connect them to the tragic past memories. The diners toast, congratulating the couple:

> Prue: Julie, Lambert. Happy anniversary.
>
> Matt: Cheers. (*They lift their glasses and drink.*) (Pinter, *Celebration* 5)

At Table two, Russell, a young banker, is dining with his attractive wife, Suki. Russell is cheating on his wife. He has an affair with a secretary and makes fun of the secretaries in front of Suki. One can see the play as a comedy of bad manners in which memory is used as a sexual twitch. Ironically, Suki the wife of a banker, also began as a plump secretary in his office, the very kind of woman that her husband is having an affair with now. The ambition for power has not changed, as in Russell's words, "These secretaries, these scrubbers love power and are just like politicians" (Pinter, *Celebration* 7). The lewd comments that Russell passes on to the secretary are also applicable to his wife. The secretaries of his office and formerly Suki have used sex as a means of gaining power. Russell now has both a wife and a scrubber (Garner 6). The dual reality of being a promiscuous secretary and a wife is embodied in one person. Suki remembers her past when she was a plump young secretary saying:

> Suki: Oh that was one when I was a plump young secretary... I could hardly walk from one cabinet to another I was so excited. (Pinter, *Celebration* 9)

The characters are acting to be ignorant. Their pretentiousness echoes musically from table to table through various memory lanes. It produces a surreal effect in the play through the usage of language. The word 'restaurant' signifies a place of high society people who are supposed to be the representative of the mainstream culture. The very embodiments of the high culture reveal superficial cultural values. They foreground artificial ideologies for future generations. They would like to see a future of wealth and celebrations. It directs the audiences to upper-class lifestyles, their slangs and incestuous relationships at home as well as at the workplace.

In Burkman's opinion, it is difficult in the play and perhaps in life as well to know whether the misogyny (who hates women) of the men calls forth the misandry (who hates men) of the women or vice versa. While the efforts of the women to emasculate the men remain somewhat sub-textual in the exchanges about the Oedipus complex, the hostility often bubbles to the surface (Burkman 5). Prue has a complaint about her husband's mother. He finds a sympathetic ear in Julie who thinks that all mothers-in-law wish to sleep with their own sons.

> Julie: All mothers-in-law are like that. They love their sons.
>
> They love their boys. They don't want their sons to be fucked by other girls. Isn't that right?
>
> Prue: Absolutely. All mothers want their sons to be fucked by themselves. (Pinter, *Celebration* 16)

After some further discussion about the desires of mothers, Lambert wants to know how old you have to be "to be fucked by your mother," to which Matt responds, "Any age, mate. Any age" (Pinter, *Celebration* 17). If one sees incest as ignorance, then the desperation grows slightly deeper. Pinter points out such incest through his characters and dialogues. Not only are the sisters married to brothers, but also, in the conversations at both tables, the oedipal thread of discussion is taken up by the three women. The guilt of incest in their relationships is frequently moving from table to table. At Table two, Russell tells Suki about his mother's bread-and-butter pudding, and Suki praises his expressiveness as poetic. She learns during this conversation that Russell's father disapproved of his poetic bent, and her diagnosis reflects the banter at Table One. He recalls his father's reactions and comments:

> Russell: I wanted to be a poet once. But I got no encouragement from my dad: he thought I was an arsehole.
>
> Suki: He was jealous of you, that's all. He saw you as a threat. He thought you wanted to steal his wife.
>
> Russell: His wife?

> Suki: Well, you know what they say.
>
> Russell: What?
>
> Suki: Oh, you know what they say. (Pinter, *Celebration* 30)

All three couples have enjoyed a night at the ballet or opera. Actually, they do not have any idea which ballet it was or why there was a lot of singing at the ballet or opera. Lambert, Julie, Prue, Matt and Russell all are taking advantage of society. They prefer money over culture and its values. The social practices are simply a display of money and superficial decadence (Garner 4). Richard, the manager, approaches their table. He asks if they have been to the theatre. Matt says they have been to the ballet, but when Richard asks what they have seen, he is greeted by the following responses:

> Richard: Very very well. Been to the play?
>
> Matt: No. The ballet.
>
> Richard: Oh the ballet? What was it?
>
> Lambert: That's a fucking good question.
>
> Matt: It's unanswerable. (Pinter, *Celebration* 19)

Julie interrupts, "What ballet?" to which Matt responds, "None of them could reach the top notes. Could they?" (Pinter, *Celebration* 20). Whether it was an opera, ballet or theatre, nobody seems to know. The characters' lack of knowledge seems less existential than absentminded; they are vacuous about anything cultural or, for that matter, about anything. If there were no such desperation in the play's subtext, one might expect these characters to turn into Ionesco's rhinoceroses at any moment (Burkman 3).

Behind such richness, they seem sexually indecent role models of the future. The theme of belonging to a wealthy culture is grounded in the character's mentality. They justify this belongingness by visiting ballets and operas, opening bottles of Franscatti and ordering dishes of Osso Bucho (Garner 3). It is the quick act of assimilation of a culture without understanding and wisdom. As for Russell, the restaurant culture is like "drowning in an ocean of richness" (Pinter, *Celebration* 29). Lambert, too, is equally transparent in his intentions when he proclaims that no one can even guess how much money he made last year.

The characters have a childhood full of domestic violence and many sexual encounters behind filing cabinets. When Lambert asks Julie how she enjoyed the food, she refuses to be impressed by the food, with the intention of offending both her husband, who is trying to please her, and Richard, who is so proud of his restaurant. Julie does not even mask her desire for Richard when she says that she'd like "to kiss him on the mouth too" (Pinter, *Celebration* 23). Prue not only tells Richard that Julie didn't like the food, but also narrates the story of how she and her sister used to listen to her "mummy beating the shit out of daddy." She exposes domestic violence, saying:

> Prue: That's how my little sister and I were brought up and she could make a better sauce than yours if she pissed into it. (Pinter, *Celebration* 22)

The well-designed interjections of the waiter become an integral part of the play to procure an in-depth understanding of relationships. The waiter's ludicrous and factually inaccurate stories serve to highlight the indulgence and self-importance of other characters. The characters have twice failed to respond and are left in silence without words as a "stratagem to cover nakedness" (qtd. in Garner 7). Waiter's first memory trip is a recount of modernist icons from Eliot to Joyce.

His interjections consist of his grandfather's stories, who had well-acquainted himself with everyone from Ezra Pound and Thomas Hardy to Clarke Gable and Al Capone, with significant contacts with Churchill and Mussolini, and thereby, the waiter claims:

> Waiter: He [his grandfather] stood four square in the centre of the intellectual and literary life of the tens, twenties and thirties. (Pinter, *Celebration* 31)

The waiter's grandfather becomes the collective symbolic narrative of European history and culture. He preserves the memory thread that can connect the celebrants to the present. The waiter shows that one could boast about the golden past of one's grandparents' or great-grandparents' times as he does in the play. One need not take it seriously and investigate it. It is enough that his mentioning of the great thinkers' names would show one's wisdom, honor and due respect for them. Pinter's waiter is more than a comic character in the play. He might have some personality disorders and is a symbol of captivity in the play. He is made to live in a memory-filled world. For Joshua Solomon, after World Wars and the Holocaust, the survivor's syndrome had been seen in patients with post-traumatic stress disorder. The patients carried a psychological imprint of the disaster, anxiety and guilt. They faced some personality changes that would persist in the rearing of the children, which Melvin Bukiet referred to as the "Second Generation" (Solomon 1). The waiter refers to the restaurant as "my womb" (Pinter, *Celebration* 33). One can consider it a reflection of what Freud called the fantasy of intra-uterine existence in psychological terms-the post-Holocaust Jewish urge to live inside one's head. The waiter can be seen as a remnant of this affected post-war generation.

Paralleling the waiter's memory trip is Lambert's memory trip. He is not using the recollections of the past as a defence but rather to attack his wife. Lambert recalls a girl whom he loved. Lambert, on the occasion of his and his wife's anniversary, thinks that it is appropriate to recall his love for another girl, who used to take "real fucking love...for walks along the river" (Pinter, *Celebration* 36). When Julie asks if she was that girl, he denies it, but she ignores this rejection and recounts her first meeting with Lambert, in counterpoint to his memories of his lost love. Prue focuses on Julie's tale and says:

> Prue: I'll never forget what you said [after meeting Lambert]. You sat on my bed. Didn't you? Do you remember?
>
> Lambert: This girl was in love with me. I'm trying to tell you.
>
> Prue: Do you remember what you said? (Pinter, *Celebration* 37)

The restaurant can be seen as a symbol of civility where everyone must look happy. It means the diners are clinically fit and behave normally. They are not suffering from any chronic illness, like Deborah of *A Kind of Alaska*, whose memory thread had been shattered. She had lost her sense of identity due to a severe mental illness. On the contrary, the celebrants are doing well in their day-to-day life. They have reconstructed their identities, adapted well to the new European culture endorsed in the market and earned a great wealth out of it. So, now, it is time to celebrate. In fact, they have created a culture of celebrations. On the surface, they are denying the past, as Rebecca did in *Ashes to Ashes*. She claimed that nothing had happened to her and to her friend and that she had no baby. The restaurant culture enacts as a suppressant of natural instincts, where characters find no psychopathic or sociopathic tendencies. They experience malice and hatred towards everyone. Russell says:

> Russell: It is a happy restaurant. For example, look at me. I'm basically a totally disordered personality, some people would describe me as a psychopath. (*to* Suki) Am I right? (Pinter, *Celebration* 39)

The sense of grand illusion of celebrations is created by Pinter through the use of excessive lavishness and luxurious lifestyle of the characters in the restaurant. But in actuality, the ambience is simultaneously deconstructed as the inner ugliness and hollowness of the elite culture become visible through the dialogues. Not much different from a dictatorship, the State was playing its well-planned game such that even a waiter, a manager or a secretary could interject in the elite class's narratives.

Pinter reveals that what was left now were mere narratives that were combating for power gain. In this culture, the power struggle does not occur at the level of conversation as such but functions at the level of an individual who attempts to assume power through interjection. One can consider it as a mere resounding of their memories. Multiple narratives wrestle under a roof, and one who is closer to the microphone can make his presence felt. The State projects that it is working for democracy—for the people, by the people and of the people. It seems that every stratum of society has a voice and space now. They all can experience equality. But in reality, one dark past is haunting each of these celebrants. Here, one can see the political resonances behind the innocent act of storytelling. While narrating, the characters are reconstructing the past, making it plausible in the present and endorsing it. All three different aspects of narration are in perfect coordination and fulfil the State's need. So, it is very simple to create a culture of merry-making acts and spot people from different stratum of society. The idea is to collaborate with them under a roof, allow them compartments according to their needs and let them work for the State.

Richard, the manager of the restaurant, interrupted the diners for his own neurotic quest for power. He is taking advantage by interrupting the symbolic mainstream narrative order of the elite class, which is considered the State's authentic narrative for the future. Without any hesitation, he enters the very act of storytelling amidst the mainstream elites. He recalls his own childhood memories of the restaurant. Richard remembers:

> Richard: Old men smoking pipes, no music of course, cheese rolls, gherkins, happiness. I think this restaurant... was inspired by that pub in my childhood. I do hope you noticed you have complimentary gherkins as soon as you take your seat. (Pinter, *Celebration* 41)

The restaurant echoes throughout the course of the play with various short memory trips of the characters. The social gathering of the restaurant, cemented with complimentary gherkins, encourages a feeling of unity and happiness that conceals the "naked aggression" (Pinter, *Celebration* 42).

The childhood memories of Richard are actually contrary to the couples' remarks about children. During the wedding anniversary celebration, they hardly talk about children as they have no real concern for them. Children have no memory and no mind. They have skulls that should be symbolically filled. Actually, their memory lanes are under construction, and their parents are playing the lead role in this act of memory formation. They are moulding their raw form of memories and manipulating them as well. One can see that the State's role is played by the institutionalisation of family units. So, whenever it means he is not part of the memory game at all. The funny remarks and mockery about children intensify the situation in the play. Prue says:

> Prue: They always loved me much more than they loved him.
>
> Julie: Me too. They loved me to distraction. I was their mother.
>
> Prue: Yes, I was too. I was my children's mother.
>
> Matt: They have no memory.
>
> Lambert: Who?
>
> Matt: Children. They have no memory. They remember nothing. They don't remember who their father was or who their mother was. It's all a hole in the wall for them. They don't remember their own life. (Pinter, *Celebration* 44)

Pinter believed that personal and political are not isolated categories. He showcases purely cultural symbols in *Celebration* to show the abuse of power. One character's memory thread triggers another's memory world, and it is presented beautifully throughout the play. Pinter captures the inevitable cacophony and dramatises it wonderfully.

In this play, Pinter revels in lewd materialism and shows how the State power works through culture. He presents the hidden cruelty in a posh society whereby the social construct is not an honest and innocent act in the form of collective remembrance but a corrupt political game. Sonia is the woman with whom Russell has had an extramarital affair. It reveals the lewdness of the elite class. She comes to the table of Lambert and Julie and says:

> Sonia: Everything all right?
>
> Julie: Perfect.
>
> Sonia: Were you at the opera this evening?
>
> Julie: No...
>
> Matt: This is a celebration... Anniversary. (Pinter, *Celebration* 44)

On Julie's mention about the anniversary, Lambert recalls how on his wedding day, he was already about to have sex at the altar and was stopped by Matt, his best man at the wedding.

> Matt: I was his best man.
>
> Lambert: I was just about to fuck her at the altar when somebody stopped me. (Pinter, *Celebration* 45)

Sonia confesses:

> Sonia: We get so many different kinds of people in here, people from all walks of life…from different countries… you don't have to speak English to enjoy good food… it's like sex…you don't have to be English to enjoy sex. (Pinter, *Celebration* 46)

Meanwhile, Sonia shares her past of having a Moroccan (not English) lover. She enters into her own past memories of a non-English lover. She laments about the past in her own grotesque style, saying:

> Sonia: I met a man from Morocco…he was very interested in sex… He's dead. He died in another woman's arms. He was on the job. Can you see how tragic my life has been? (Pinter, *Celebration* 47)

Sonia has shared her tragic past with the diners. They pay her lip services and participate in her memory trips. She greets them and moves away. For Lambert, she is a lovely woman. Then, the waiter comes and pours the wine into their glasses. The waiter asks formally about interjecting their conversation:

> Waiter: Do you mind if I interject…I heard you saying something about the Hollywood studio system in the thirties…you might be interested to know that my grandfather was very familiar with a lot of the old Hollywood film stars… Clark Gable and Elisha Cook Jr and he was one of the very few native-born Englishmen… with Hedy Lamarr.
>
> Julie: No…
>
> Waiter: …was a well-established Irish Mafia in Hollywood in those days… Irish film stars…Irish gangsters in Chicago…John Dillinger the celebrated gangsters and Gary Cooper the celebrated film star…were Jewish.
>
> *Silence*. (Pinter, *Celebration* 50)

From time to time, the waiter interrupts the flow of the conversations, and through many interjections, he interlinks the disjointed memory frames of the celebrants. One can say that he uses cultural memory as a frame to gather the people in the lavish restaurant. He mentions great names during the act of interruption. To some extent, he carries and offers the so-called golden past along with costly wine bottles. The references made by the waiter trigger a series of diners' past experiences. His second memory trip of linking the movie stars and mafia is directed towards Lambert and Matt, who are, in reality, strategy consultants. It opens up many past links of the diners' lives, as afterward, Lambert tells Julie:

> Lambert: You see that girl at that table?... I fucked her when she was eighteen...
>
> Julie: What, by the banks of the river? (Pinter, *Celebration* 50)

The girl whom Lambert points out is Suki, Russell's wife. Lambert waves at Suki, and she waves back. She whispers to her husband to stand up and move to Lambert's table, and Russell follows her. They all greet each other. They seem more than happy to see each other and make public acquaintances. They update their past memories, recalling minor past obsessions, like love lives, gardening, love for flowers, for girls' bums and filling cabinets. Then, they all slip to their social and professional concerns and jobs. They converse about vague topics, such as Suki's school teaching, Julie and Prue's charity works, bankers and finally revealing that Lambert and Matt are strategy consultants. Their job is to enforce peace. They seem close kin to the agents of the state-power. Matt declares:

> Matt: We're peaceful strategy consultants.
>
> Lambert: Worldwide. Keeping the peace. (Pinter, *Celebration* 60)

The characters are new custodians of power, gradually shifting from being old-moneyed colonialists to newly powerful businessmen. This transition shows a reordering of the hierarchy of power, which due, to the deregulations of the money markets of the 1980s, has created great wealth for a well-placed few (Garner 3). Pinter shows Lambert and Matt as strategy consultants who are involved worldwide in keeping the peace. They have made a good deal of money out of it. Being strategy consultants, their job is to bring peace to British shores. They have better plans for European culture—to fill the minds with wealth and create a culture of celebrations. They are the architects of the culture. The drama of civility is not restricted to a mere high-class restaurant, opera house and ballet. It is extended too far for Prue and Julie's charity works and for Matt and Lambert's occupations as peacemakers in society.

The conversation is again interrupted by the waiter. In his third speech, the waiter portrays his grandfather as an altruistic saint. Pinter used the language just as a sheath to cover the psychological nudity of minds. The waiter's stories are absurd and fact-wise inaccurate. They serve to highlight the indulgence and self-importance of other characters. The characters looked deaf to the waiter. They have failed to respond and are left in a sense of silence without their words. In the end, when dinners are over, in waiter's soliloquy, the grandfather suddenly appears as a real character:

> Waiter: When I was a boy my grandfather used to take me to the edge of the cliffs and we'd look out to sea. He bought me a telescope. I don't think they have telescopes anymore. I used to look through this telescope and sometimes I'd see a boat. The boat would grow bigger through the telescopic lens. Sometimes I'd see people on the boat. A man, sometimes, and a woman, or sometimes two men. The sea glistened. (Pinter, *Celebration* 72)

The telescope, cliffs and sea evoke Pinter's and the whole Jewish race's memories of the past. The memories are oscillating inside painfully, but there is no escape. Pinter's waiter further leads on memory trips—a symbolic memory world. In the end, he explores the poetic mystery of life, saying:

> Waiter: My grandfather introduced me to the mystery of life and I'm still in the middle of it. I can't find the door to get out. My grandfather got out of it. He got right out. He left behind him and he didn't look back...he got that absolutely right. (Pinter, *Celebration* 72)

The reference to the mystery of life can be related to the process of birth and death. For Burkman, the issue of birth and death reverberates everywhere in *Celebration*. It is a symbol of the narrative order of human life. The play describes celebration, which can be seen as a kind of displacement where the act of mourning (death) is displaced into the very act of celebration (birth). In *The Birthday Party*, Stanley hides out from life at a seaside boarding house but is terrified of the destruction as Goldberg and McCann insist on celebrating his birthday. In *A Kind of Alaska*, Deborah is told of her upcoming birthday celebration, but she fears she will not be able to keep her presents herself. In each play, as in *Celebration*, there is a pre-oedipal desire to return to the womb or to hide out from life and a terrible fear of death. The waiter compares his grandfather to Jesus Christ and introduces him as a deity in restaurant culture by presenting him to be present everywhere and knowing everything. It is he who has found the door and unlocked the riddle of human existence (Burkman 11). Grandfather introduces the mystery of life as King Lear's offer to Cordelia to "take upon mystery of things" (qtd. in Billington 406). The waiter's final interjection is interrupted by Lambert. He ignores the waiter verbally and physically by standing and congratulating Richard on the dinner, followed by an excessive tip. The play ends with the waiter alone on the stage, saying, "And I'd like to make further interjection" (Pinter, *Celebration* 72). But who was he talking to remains a riddle. Whether he was interacting with the audience or imaginary diners? No one can be sure about his memory-filled world. It exists either inside his imagination or outside in the real world.

5
Conclusion

Harold Pinter's memory theatre becomes an archive of hidden as well as revealed knowledge about the past and its haunting presence. His plays are vivid experiments in abstraction and aestheticism. They provide an ironic treatment of institutions of State, religion and ethics. They explore the ambiguity of human lives in reality. Drama as a genre is an act of remembrance and memory process. Pinter has achieved perfection in exhibiting this process in his memory plays. Human beings can be considered as embodiments of their past memories. By narrating the past tales, they want to authenticate their existence. To memorise is to search for an identity. Past memories generate a comparative area where the present life of the characters is constantly under scrutiny. Who, when and how can one narrate one's tale of life is politicised by the power of the State or gender through narration. It signifies that identities are created by the power of narrative.

Ironically, Pinter's memory plays show an anti-authoritarian stance on people's past and identity. The character's obsession with memory can be considered as a craving for lost identity, space and existence. The plays reflect Pinter's own longing for a Jewish identity, which was badly injured in war trauma and tortured during the Jewish Holocaust. Pinter deals with human isolation and the crucial problem of communication through the characters' attempts to recall the past. The plays undertaken in the thesis have a static quality and signify mental paralysis. Their struggle for power is prevalent in routine life. The characters are constantly bombarded with invasions and intruders threatening their lives. They are trapped in a vicious circle of losing the battle and fighting for physical and mental territory. Through the ever-changing nature of memories, an insecure world becomes visible in which the desire for security, command and communication is always shattered. Memory always carries with it the prevalence of past, present and future. Pinter established the memory-making process that provides legitimacy to the existence of the characters. The present then becomes a platform to illustrate both what is remembered and what is deliberately forgotten.

The most painful aspect of Pinter's own experience of evacuation during World War II and especially the Holocaust is the loss of identity and the sense of residing in an in-between world. Pinter and his friends confronted the most terrible period of the history of German Jews. Pinter's obsession begins with the occurrence of fascism in the post-war East End world. It was a kind of revival of fascism. Anyone born and brought up in East End endured social and racial tensions. In the 1920s, the Hackney Gazette fulminated against the presence of 30,000 Jews and others (qtd. in Billington 17). They deprived the locals of their jobs and lodges. The racial prejudices appeared in the form of Oswald Mosley's British Union of Fascists campaign against Anglo-Jewry. Later in 1934, racial segregation had become a party policy. Morris Beckman, in his book *The 43 Group*, painted an ugly picture of the aftermaths of War and the Holocaust. Both the onlookers and victims in Pinter's drama, who grew up under the shadow of the Shoah (in Hebrew, it means calamity, twentieth-century Holocaust), recognised the commonality of suffering in countless stories they had heard. Pinter's characters are denizens of some past and alienated world disconnected from the present world.

The study is based on modern critical theory and its other aspects found in cultural studies and historiography. An attempt has been made to configure the omnipresent nature of memory in Pinter's drama. The work elaborates upon the cultural value of memory and its relationship with history, cultural studies and politics from a personal to the national level that formed the very core of the Jewish people. It involves complicated interactions of personal memory, social memory and resulting politics of cultural memory. By using cultural memory as a decisive tool, one can examine how the Holocaust has affected the whole of the Jewish race in general and Pinter's characters in particular.

This research project focused on the analysis of cultural memory in some of Harold Pinter's plays. Memories are the events that have actually happened and histories are the subjective representations of what States believe and historians write for the States. In order to understand the past, one should analyze actual historical documentation and also take into account personal reverberations. Memory is the secret through which cultures or people ensure their traditional continuum. Memories, with the aid of collective knowledge, construct the cultural identity of the people from generation to generation. Repeated references to the whole lived past validate the members of a society of their cultural identity. The act of recalling, especially the tragic past, supplies the people with an awareness of their unity in time and space. As a result, a historical consciousness of a common past is generated. It also becomes proof of the Jewish existence from the past times to the present moment and fulfils the narrative order of their lives. They feel it is worth living for and adore a communal sense of living. For the oppressed or minorities, cultural memory works like a resisting force to face the pressure of mainstream society and its rigidities. The thesis includes a detailed study of cultural memory, its role in identity formation and how it becomes a memory culture of Holocaust memories through memorials, print media and other art forms. Later, the memories were used as political tools for taking advantage of personal recollections of past events.

Pinter's plays, *Old Times*, *No Man's Land* and *Betrayal*, project how past memories can become tools of exploitation for gaining a psychic advantage over the masses. The chapter titled 'Obsession with Memory' analysed the obsession with memory and its proportional relationship with the fear of forgetting the past. For Jews, the Nazi brutality was enough to throw life out of gear. The Jewish narrative lost its trace in the time and space continuum. The State constructed collective memories in the form of commemorations. The political leaders narrated the past for their own benefit. A group's cultural memory, projected in Pinter's drama, elaborated upon the equation between periphery and centre that shaped post-war European culture. In *Old Times*, *No Man's Land* and *Betrayal*, the characters resided under constant fear of the "knock at the door" (Billington 82). The cultural memory of war existed in the dark recesses of the characters' minds. The obsession with remembering and recalling past events exhibited a quest for something substantial that could trace an identity. In the plays, the obsession is nostalgia for the past that transforms into a persistent fear of oblivion.

In Pinter's drama, one can observe a kind of cultural neurosis after the World Wars and the Holocaust in particular. The events have become an inseparable part of his memory. He directly approaches the collective remembrance and, at the same time, reveals the underlying political façade behind commemoration. Pinter showcases that cultural memory has a definitive sense of historical consciousness. One can see that Pinter's characters often repeat rather than recall the past.

The characters have inherited a past through oral and written accounts and narratives. People never select painful past events like the Holocaust except for observing mourning ceremonies. The fact is that the terror of trauma exists because painful memories have their own survival time. Pinter deals not with the memories of survivors but with their effect on people, especially Jews, who have not only been directly touched by the horrors but also are sensitive enough to be scarred by them for life. Pinter succeeds in relating his own curiosity about the role of memory and its relevance in dealing with the trauma of the Holocaust. The practice of remembrance provided a new commercial aspect to the already circulating war memories. The State utilised cultural memory to evoke the frozen moments of the past and give them a direction and shape for political benefits.

The fourth chapter, titled 'Cultural Memory and Politics', deals with the knotted and jinxed love stories as embodiments of the brutality of State power. Power always tries to build a justifiable narrative of the past that legitimises its deeds to its people. A nation can remember through its people what it wants its people to remember. After the catastrophes, the authorities were bent on projecting the revival of Europe. It created a false hope for a better utopian world, where stability and prosperity prevailed. The strategy could only work if prosperity were seen around. The State wanted to reinstate the golden past (State's golden history) and make people participants by indulging them in merry-making acts. The war memories moulded the national memory, history and the collective memory of the masses in Europe. The memory remnants of the World Wars were sold by the State. The cultural memories were transformed into sellable objects, such as films, books, articles, photographs, souvenirs, letters, memoirs, media and particularly war cinema. War history was sold in the form of biographies and autobiographies of the victims and victimizers alike.

Pinter's plays projected perverted love stories, full of arbitrariness and abuse of power. The power of cultural memory resides in the conscious decision to choose the particular memories to pass on for future design. Those in a position to rule definitely choose a common pool of memories, circulate it among the people and make it accessible. They raise it in celebrations and create harmony in society. Pinter has proved successful in making the full use of cultural memory and its articulation in politics through broken syntax, characters' psyche, incoherent memory trips and subject matter. Additionally, he interrogates how identity could be preserved in the form of cultural memory. Pinter has painted a real picture of society, its social/cultural memory and its various practices in society through his memory plays. He raises challenging questions about how such shattered memories can produce reliable identities and growing societies. He observes how such a fluid sense of self can become sharp State political tools to gain an advantage.

His characters are entrapped in a remote past, as is revealed in *Old Times*. They lived on an emotional island that has been frozen forever like *No Man's Land*. They are consistently betraying each other under imposed fascist oppression, which is evident in his play *Betrayal*. The characters are caught in their own mental zones, which are exactly portrayed in *A Kind of Alaska*, where one can see different entities of time, the past-present-future, on stage. The characters are living in transitory phases. *Moonlight* is symbolic of a borrowed or deflected light rather than a real source of illumination where everything is crystal clear. The characters are stepped back into the dim light phase of memory, which is full of ghostly appearances. They had no sense of falsity and truth. They had nothing to carry forward but mere acts of futile repetitions. *Ashes to Ashes* reveals the futile digging in the past and an act of investigating the separate entities of life. Pinter and his characters arise from the ashes of the Holocaust and invite the audiences to celebrate the horrors in an oblique sense. His last play *Celebration* produces an irony over the culture of celebrations in Europe. The character's desperation to return to the womb or any secure place directs the audiences toward their past Holocaust experiences.

This project is a study of his seven plays in seven different phases as correlated seven acts of the scarred human psyche's growth in the form of memory plays in chronological order. It is also a narrative of the growth or evolution of Pinter and his folk. Man has a tremendous power of memory, which can neither be created nor destroyed by outer forces easily. Yet, it can be scarred, manipulated and injured. In spite of the hurdles, cultural memory has a regenerating power. In post-Holocaust Europe, a stage had come when there was nobody to carry forward the burden of these brutal acts. The State had started to exonerate itself through the commemoration processes. Pinter made sure that cultural memory should stay alive through dramatic art. Through his corpus, the reverberations of the Holocaust continue to haunt the world to date. Who cares if the State (Hitler) has plotted a bloody hell for Jews or other minorities? Pinter removes the façade of European civility and superiority by producing the spectres of the Holocaust. Pinter's memory plays explore past situations with immense intensity.

Pinter thrills the audiences with words and actions and creates a compulsory condition to look back into the past corridors of European history once more for investigation.

Bibliography

Works by Harold Pinter

Pinter, Harold. *A Kind of Alaska*. London, Faber & Faber, 1982.

———. *Ashes to Ashes*. London, Faber & Faber, 1996.

———. *Betrayal*. London, Faber & Faber, 1978.

———. *Celebration and The Room*. London, Faber & Faber, 2000.

———. *Harold Pinter: Plays VI*. London, Faber & Faber, 1998.

———. *Moonlight*. London, Faber & Faber, 1993.

———. *No Man's Land*. London, Faber & Faber, 1975.

———. "Nobel Lecture." *The Nobel Prize*, 19 Mar. 2012,, https://www.nobelprize.org/prizes/literature/2005/pinter/lecture/.

———. *Old Times*. London, Faber & Faber, 1971.

———. *Play One: The Birthday Party, The Room, The Dumb Waiter, A Slight Ache, A Night Out, The Hothouse, The Examination*. London, Faber & Faber, 1991.

———.*Play Two: The Caretaker, The Dwarfs, The Collection, The Lover, Night School, Last to Go, Special Offer.* London, Faber & Faber, 1996.

———. *Play Three: The Homecoming, Tea Party, The Basement, Landscape, Silence, Old Times, No Man's Land*. London, Faber & Faber, 1996.

———. *Plays Four: Betrayal, Monologue, One for the Road, Mountain Language, Family Voices, A Kind of Alaska, Victoria Station, Moonlight, Ashes to Ashes.*, London, Faber & Faber, 1998.

———. *Poems and Prose, 1949–1977*. London, Eyre Methuen, 1978.

———. *Press Conference*. London, Faber & Faber, 2002.

———. *Remembrance of Things Past*. London, Faber & Faber, 2000.

———. *The Art of Theatre III, Interview With L.M. Bensky*. Paris Review, Autumn 1966, pp. 31.

———. *The Proust Screenplay*. London, Faber & Faber, 2001.

———. *The Kurds Have Lifted the Veil*. The Guardian, 1999.

———. *The NATO Actin in Serbia*. London, Verso, 2000.

———. *Various Voices 1948–2005*. London, Faber & Faber, 2005.

———. *War*. London, Faber & Faber, 2003.

———. *Writing For The Theatre. Play: One*. London, Methuen, 1983.

———. *Writing for Myself. Plays: Two*. London, Faber & Faber, 1996.

Secondary Sources

Adorno, Theodor W. *Can We Live After Auschwitz? A Philosophical Reader*, edited by Rolf Tiedman. Stanford, Stanford 2003.

Almansi, Guido, and Henderson S. *Harold Pinter*. London, Methuen, 1983.

Alonso, Ana Maria. "The Effects of Truth: Pre-representation of the Past and the Imagination of the Community." *Journal of Historical Sociology*, 1988, pp. 33–57.

Anderson, Michael. *Anger and Detachment: A Study of Arden, Osborne and Pinter*. London, Pitman Publishing, 1976.

Appleyard, Bryan. *The New Light That Burns Within Harold Pinter*. The Times, 1984.

Aragay, Mireia. "Writing Politics, and Ashes to Ashes: An Interview With Harold Pinter. Florida, University of Tampa, 1996, pp. 4–15.

———. *Pinter Politics and Postmodernism*. Cambridge, Cambridge University Press, 2001.

Armstrong, Raymond. *Kafka and Pinter: Shadow Boxing*. St. Martin's Press, 1999.

Assmann, Aleida. *Memory Individual and Collective. The Oxford Handbook of Contextual Political Analysis*, edited by Robert E.G. and Charles Tilly. Oxford, Oxford University Press, 2006, pp. 210–24.

Assmann, Jan. "Collective Memory and Cultural Identity." *New German Critique*, 65 Spring, 1995, pp. 124–35.

Atwood, Margret. *Pinteresque in the Pinter Review: Collected Essays. 1999–2000*, edited by Francis Gillen and Steven H. Gale. Florida: University of Tampa Press, 2000.

Baker, W., and Tabachnick. *Harold Pinter*. Edinburgh: Oliver Boyd, 1973. Bakewell, Joan. *In an Empty Bandstand.* Listener, June 1980, pp. 11.

Bartlett, F.C. *Remembering*. Cambridge, Cambridge University Press, 1932.

Batty, Mark. *About Pinter: The Playwright & the Work*. London, Faber & Faber, 2005.

Bauderlaire, Charles. *Selected Writings on Art and Literature.* Penguin Books, 1992.

Becker, Carl. "Annual Address of the President of the American Historical Association." *American Historical Review*, no. 37, Jan. 1932, pp. 221–36.

Belli, Robert F., et al. "The Misremembering of Important Past Events." *American Association for Public Opinion Research Conference*, Louderdale, 1995.

Benjamin, Walter. *The Story-teller. Illuminations*, edited by Hannah Arendt, New York, Harcourt Brace and World, 1995, pp. 167–96.

Bennet, Leslie. "On Films Pinter's Betrayal Displays New Subtelties." *New York Times*, 27 Feb. 1983, p. 123.

Bennet, T. *'Stored Virtue: Memory, the Body and the Evolutionary Museum' Memory Cultures, Memory, Subjectivity and*

Recognition. New Brunswick & London, Transaction Publishers, 2006.

Bensky, Lawrence M. *Harold Pinter in Theatre at Work*. London, Methuen, 1967, pp. 96–109.

Bermond, Claude. "The Logic of Narrative Possibilities." *New Literary History*, vol. 11, no. 3, 1980, pp. 387–412.

Billington, M. *Harold Pinter*. London, Faber & Faber, 2007.

———. *The Evil That Men Do*. The Guardian, 30 Jun. 2001.

Bhabha, Homi K., editor. *Nation and Narration*. New York, Routledge, 1990.

———. *The Location of Culture*. London, Routledge, 1994.

Bloch, Maurice E.F. *How We Think: Anthropological Approaches to Cognition, Memory and Literacy*. Boulder, Westview Press, 1998.

Blow, David. *Hackney's Empire*. Waterstone's New Books Christmas, 1990, pp. 46–7.

Bogacz, Ted. *War Neurosis and Cultural Change in England*, 1914–22. *Journal of Contemporary History*, 1989, pp. 18–25.

Bold, Alan, editor. *Harold Pinter.* London, Vision and Barnes and Noble, 1986.

Bosworth, Patricia. "Why Does He Write More?" *New York Times*, 27 Oct. 1968, p. 3.

Bouwsma W.J. *A Usable Past: Essay in European Cultural History*. California, Berkeley University of California Press, 1990.

Boyarin, Jonathan, editor. *Remapping Memory: The Politics of Timespace*. Minneapolis, University of Minnesota Press, 1994.

Braudy, Leo. *Narrative Form in History and Fiction*. Princeton, Princeton University Press, 1970.

Brockmeier, Jens. *Remembering and Forgetting: Narrative as Cultural Memory*. http:// cap.sagepub.com.content.8/1/15. Accessed 14 Apr. 2012.

Brook, Peter. *The Empty Space*. London, Pelican, 1972.

Brown, John Russell, editor. *Modern British Dramatists: New Perspectives*. Englewood, New Jersey, Prentice-Hall, 1984.

Brown, Kenneth. "Polish Jews in Paris: The Ethnography of Memory." *American Anthropologist*, 1995, pp. 239.

Brown, Richard. *Society as a Text*. Chicago, University of Chicago Press, 1987.

———. "The Position of the Narrative in Contemporary Society." *New Literary History*, vol. 11, no. 3, Spring 1980, pp. 545–50.

Bruner, Jerome. "Life as a Narrative." *Social Research*, vol. 54, no. 1, Spring 1987, pp. 11–32.

———. "The Narrative Construction of Reality." *Critical Enquiry*, vol. 18, no. 1, Autumn 1991, pp. 1–21.

Burkman, K.H. *The Dramatic World of Harold Pinter*. New York, Ohio State University Press, 1971.

———. Harold Pinter's *Ashes to Ashes: Rebecca and Devlin as Albert Speer*. Tampa, University of Tampa, Spring 1998, pp. 86–96.

Burke, Peter. *Facets of Cultural History*. Cambridge, Polity Press, 2003.

Butler, Thomas, editor. *Memory: History, Culture and the Mind*. Oxford, Basil Blackwell, 1990.

Carr, David. "Narrative and the Real World: An Argument for Continuity." Vol. 25, no. 2, 1986, pp. 117–31.

———. *Time, Narrative and History*. Bloomington, Indiana University Press, 1986.

Carty, Ciaran. "Citizen Pinter." *Sunday Tribune*, 1 May 1994.

Cathy, Caruth, editor. *Trauma: Exploration in Memory*. Baltimore: Hopkins University Press, 1995.

Cavander, Kenneth, et al. *Behind the Scenes: Theatre and Film Interviews from Transatlantic Review*, edited by Joseph F. McCrindle, London, Pitman, 1971, pp. 209–21.

Clendinnen, Olga. *Reading the Holocaust*. Cambridge, Cambridge University Press, 1994.

Cohn, Ruby. *Currents in Contemporary Drama*. Bloomington, Indiana University Press, 1969.

Collingwood, R. G. *The Idea of History*. Oxford, Clarendon Press, 1946.

Connerton, Paul. *How Societies Remember.* Cambridge, Cambridge University Press, 1989.

Csordas, Thomas J, editor. *Embodiment and Experience: The Existential Ground of Culture and Self*. Cambridge, Cambridge University Press, 1994.

Crites, Stephen. "The Narrative Quality of Experience." *Journal of the American Academy of Religion*, vol. ix, no. 3, Sept. 1971, pp. 291–311.

———. *Storytime: Recollecting the Past and Projecting the Future. Narrative Psychology*, edited by Theodore Sarbin, New York, Praeger, 1986, pp. 152–73.

Dan, Todman. *The Great War: Myth and Memory*. London, Hambledon and London, 2005.

Daniel L., Schachter. *Memory Distortion: How Minds Brains and Societies Reconstruct the Past*, Cambridge, Harvard University Press, 1995.

Dave, Irvin. *Rouge Theatre*. 2 Mar. 2011, http://www.tucsonsentinel.com/arts/report/0330211-oldtimesreview/Pinter-old-times-sisyphean-search-truth.

Davis, Charles. *Body as Spirit: The Nature of Religious Feeling*. New York, Seabury Press, 1976.

Deray, W.H. "On the Role of Narrative in Historiography." *History and Theory*, vol. 10, 1971, pp. 23–42.

Dussel, Enrique. *Ethics and the Theology of Liberation*, translated by Bernard F. McWilliams. Maryknoll, New York, Orbis Books, 1978.

Dukore, Bernard F. *Harold Pinter*. London, The Macmillan Press, Ltd., 1982.

———. *Where Laughter Stops: Pinter's Tragicomedy*. Columbia, University of Missouri Press, 1976.

Edwards, David. *Unthinkable Thoughts*. Santa Monica Review, Spring 2000.

Edward, Sydney. *Pinter's Taxi to No Man's Land*. Evening Standard, 11 Jul. 1976.

Ekstein, Modris. *The Great War and the Birth of Modern Age*. Boston, Houghton Mifflin, 1989.

Eslom, John. *Post-War British Theatre*. London, Routledge, 1981.

Esslin, Martin. *Pinter the Playwright*. London, Methuen, 1982.

———. *The Field of Drama*. London, Methuen, 1987.

———. *The Peopled Wound: The Plays of Harold Pinter.* London, Methuen & Co. Ltd., 1970.

———. *The Theatre of Absurd*. New York, Penguin Books, 1983.

Evans, B. *A Short History of English Drama*. Harmondsworth, Penguin, 1948.

Falck, Colin. *Myth, Truth, and Literature*. Cambridge, Cambridge University Press, 1989.

Faulk, Sebastian. *Birdsong*. London, Hutchinson, 1993.

Fisher, Walter. *Human Communication as Narration*. Columbia, University of South Carolina Press, 1987.

Ford, Anna. *Radical Departures*. Listeners, 27 Oct. 1988.

Fortier, Ted. *Religion and Resistance in the Encounter Between Coeur d'Alene Indians and Jesuit Missionaries*. New York, Mellen, 2002.

Frassica, Pietro, editor. *Primo Levi as Witness: Proceedings of a Symposium Held in Princeton University, April 30–May 2, 1989*. Fiesole, Casalini, 1990.

Freud, S. *Art and Literature*. Penguin Books, 1990.

———. *Civilization and Its Discontents*, translated by Joan Riviere, Chandigarh: Abhishek Publications, 1978.

———. *New Introductory Lectures on Psychoanalysis*, translated by W.J.H. Sportt, 2nd ed., London, Hogarth Press, 1937.

Foucault, Michel. *The Archaeology of Knowledge*. London & New York, Routledge, 2002.

Furet, Francois. “From Narrative History to History as Problem.” *Diogenes*, no. 89, Spring 1975, pp. 106–23.

Fussell, Paul. *The Great War and Modern Memory*. Oxford, Oxford University Press, 1975.

Gale, John. *Taking Pains With Pinter*. Observer, 16 Jun. 1962, p. 19.

Gale, Steven H. *Harold Pinter: Critical Approaches*. London, Associated, University Presses, 1986.

———. Sharp-Cut: *Harold Pinter's Screenplays and the Artistic Process*. Lexington, University of Kentucky Press, 2003.

———. *The Pinter Review*. Thampa: University of Thampa Press, 2004.

Garner, Naomi. *Politics of Harold Pinter*. Dec.sss 2012, vol. 4, http://www.studentpulse.com/articles/616/4/the-politics-of-harold-pinter. Accessed 4 Jan. 2013.

Gascoigne, Bamber. *Twentieth Century Drama*. London, Hutchinson, 1962.

Geetz, Clifford. *The Interpretation of Cultures*. New York, Basic Books, 1988.

Gergen, Kenneth and Mary Gergen. “The Social Construction of Narrative Accounts.” *Historical Social Psychology*, 1984, pp. 173–89.

Ghiraldi and Sierz. *Pinter and Pinteresque*. 1997, http://www.inyerface-theatre.com/archive15.html. Accessed 2 Jan. 2013.

Glanville, Brian. “I am a Jew Who Writes.” *Jewish Chronicle*, 11 Mar. 1960.

Gombrich, Earnst H. *Aby Warburg: An Intellectual Biography*. Chicago, University, of Chicago Press, 1986.

Goldberg, Michael. *Theology and Narrative: A Critical Introduction*. Nashville, Abingdon Press, 1982.

Goldman, Susan, and Connie Varnhagen. “Memory for Embedded and Sequential Story Structures.” *Journal of Memory and Language*, vol. 25, Aug. 1986, pp. 401–18.

Goodrich, F. & Albert. *The Diary of Anne Frank*. New York, Random House, 1956.

Grant, Steve. *Pinter: My Plays, my Polemics, my Pad*. Independent, 20 Sept. 1993.

Gray, Simon. *An Unnatural Pursuit*. London, Faber & Faber, 1985.

Greig, Geordie. *You Talking to Me*? Tatler, Aug. 2004, pp. 108–13.

Gross, Miriam. *Pinter on Pinter*. Observer, 5 Oct. 1980, pp. 25.

Gussow, Mel. *Conversation With Pinter*. London, Nick Hern, 1994.

Gusset, Ortega. *History as a System*. New York, Norton, 1941, pp.166.

Halbwachs, Maurice. *The Collective Memory*. New York, Harper, 1980.

———. *On Collective Memory*, translated by Lewis Coser, Chicago: University of, Chicago Press, 1992.

Hall, Adam. *The Berlin Memorandum*. Collins, 1965.

Hall, Ann C. *A Kind of Alaska: Women in the Plays of O'Neill, Pinter and Shepard*. Carbondale & Edwardsville: Southern Illinois University Press, 1993.

Hall, Peter. *Exposed by the Mask*. London: Oberon, 2000.

Hamerow, Theodore. "The Bureaucratization of History." *American Historical Review*, vol. 94, no. 3, 1989, pp. 654–60.

Hardy, Barbara. "Towards a Poetics of Fiction: An Approach Through Narrative." *Novel: A Forum on Fiction*, vol. 35, Spring 1988, pp. 99–130.

Hern, Nick. *A Play and Its Politics: One for the Road*. London: Methuen, 1985,, pp. 5–24.

Higgonet, Margret R. *Nurses at the Front: Writing the Wounds of the Great War*. Boston: Northeastern University Press, 2001.

Himmelfarb, Gertrude. *Is It a Plot?* New York Times Book Review, 1994, pp. 41.

———. *The New History and the Old.* Cambridge, Harvard University Press, 1987.

Hinchman, Lewis P, and Sandra K Hinchman. *Memory ,Identity and Community: The Idea of Narrative in the Human Sciences.* Albany, New York Press, 2001.

Hirsch, Herbert. *Genocide and the Politics of Memory.* Chap Hill and London: North Carolina Press, 1995.

Hirsch, Maurice. *Family Pictures: Maus, Mourning and Post-Memory Discourse.* Theatrical Studies in Media and Culture. 1993, pp. 3–29.

Homer, Frederic D. *Primo Levi and the Politics of Survival.* Columbia, University of Missouri Press, 2001.

Horowitz, M. J., editor. *Essential Papers on Post Traumatic Stress Disorder.* New York, New York University Press, 1999.

Horney, K. *The Neurotic Personality of Our Time.* London: Broadway House, 1937.

Hunt, Lynn, editor. *The New Cultural History.* Berkeley, University of California Press, 1989.

Huyssen, Andreas. “The Wounds of Berlin.” *Critical Inquiry,* vol. 24, no. 1, 1997, pp. 57–81.

Hynes, Samuel. *A War Imagined: The First World War and English Culture.* New York: Atheneum, 1991.

———. *The Soldiers’ Tale: Bearing Witness to Modern War.* New York, A. Lane, 1997.

Inenberg, Noah. *Between Redemption and Doom: The Strains of German-Jewish Modernism.* Lincoln, University of Nebraska Press, 1999.

Irvin-Zaecki, Iwona. *Frames of Remembrance: The Dynamics of Cultural Memory.* New Brunswick, New Jersey, Transaction, 1994.

Jackson, Bernard. *Narrative Theories and Legal Discourse.* New York: Routledge, 1990.

Jameson, Frederic. *The Political Unconscious: Narrative as a Society Symbolic Act*. Ithaca, Cornell University Press, 1981.

Jayne, Blanchord. *Old Times: Review*. dctheatrescene.com/2011/5/25/old-times/.

Jeanett Rodriguez, *Ted Fortier. Cultural Memory: Resistance, Faith and Identity*. Austin, University of Texas Press, 2007.

Jeffreys, Daniel. 2–7 Apr. 2007, htttp://www.onlinereview London.com/reviews/OldTimes.html. Accessed 11 Aug. 2007.

Jelin, Elizabeth. *State Repression and Labours of Memory*. Minneapolis, Minnesota, University of Minnesota Press, 2003.

Johnstone, Barbara. *Stories, Community and Place*. Bloomington, Indiana University Press, 1990.

John, Russell. *Anger and After*. London, Penguin, 1962.

Jones, Edwards T. "Harold Pinter: A Conversation." *Literature/ Film Quarterly*, vol. 21, 1993. pp. 3–9.

Jonson, B.S. *Evacuees, The Pinter Review: Collected Essays 1993–94*. Florida, University of Tampa Press, 1994, pp. 8–13.

Jung, Carl. *Modern Man in Search of Soul*, translated by W.S. Dell and Cary F. Baynes, America, USA Press, 1933.

———. *Psychological Types or Psychology of Individuation*, translated H.G., Baynes, London, Routledge, 1923.

Kaplan, Marion. *The Making of Jewish Middle Class*. New York, Oxford University Press, 1991.

Keen, Ernest. "Narrative Construction in Treating Multiple Personality Disorder." *Journal of Psychology and Life History*, vol. 5, no. 3, 1995, pp. 247–53.

Keightley, Emily. *Engaging With Memory*. Edinburgh, Edinburgh Press, 2008.

Kemp, Peter. "History as Narrative and Practice. (Interview With Paul Ricoeur).", *Philosophy Today*, vol. 29, 1985, pp. 1–29.

Kirmayer, Laurence J. *Landscape of Memory: Trauma, Narrative and Dissociation in Tense Past: Cultural essays in Trauma and Memory*, edited by Paul Antze And Michael Lambeks. London, Routledge, (1996), pp. 173–78.

Klein, Joanne. *Making Pictures: The Pinter Screenplays*. Columbus: State University Press, 1985.

Klein, Kerwin Lee. "On the Emergence of Memory in Historical Discourse." *Representations*, 69, Winter 2000, pp. 127–50.

Kluitenberg, Eric. "The Politics of Cultural Memory." 10 Jan. 2023, http://www.aughty.org. Accessed 10 Jan. 2023.

Knapp, Steven. "Collective Memory and the Actual Past." *Representations*, Spring 1989, pp. 134–47.

Knowles, Ronald. *Understanding of Harold Pinter*. Columbia: University of South Carolina, 1995.

Kurtz, Donald V. "The Virgin of Guadalupe and the Politics of Becoming Human." *Journal of Anthropological Research*, Summer 1982, pp. 192–210.

Lahr, John. "The Theatre - Harold Pinter's Ashes to Ashes." *The New Yorker*, 1999, http://www. newyorker.com. Accessed 10 Apr. 2012.

Lacan, Jacques. "The Neurotic's Individual Myth." *Psychoanalytical Quarterly*, vol. 48,, 1979, pp. 405–25.

Landau, Misia. "Human Evolution as Narrative." *American Scientist*, vol. 72, 1982,, pp. 262–68.

Lagrou, Pieter. *The Legacy of Nazi Occupation: Patriotic Memory and National, Recovery in Western Europe, 1945–65*. Cambridge, Cambridge University Press, 2000.

Langer, Lawrence. *Holocaust Testimonies*. New Haven: Yale University Press, 1991.

Lanqueur, Thomas W. *Names, Bodies and the Anxiety of Erasure in the Social and Political Body*, edited by R Theodore and Wolfgang Natter, New York: Guilford Press, 1996, pp. 123–44.

Levi, Primo. *The Drowned and the Saved*. New York: Summit Books, 1988.

———. *Survival in Auschwitz: The Nazi Assault on Humanity*, translated by Stuart Woolf, New York, Summit Books, 1986.

Lewis, Pierce. "The Future of Our Past: Our Clouded Vision of Historic Preservation." *Pioneer American*, 1975, pp. 1–20.

Lees, Peter. *Shell Shock: Traumatic Neurosis and the British Soldiers of the First World, War*. New York, Palgrave, 2002.

Linde, Charlotte. "Private Stories in Public Discourse: Narrative Analysis in the Social Sciences." *Poetics*, vol. 15, 1986, pp. 183–202.

Luckmann, Thomas. *Remarks on Personal Identity: Inner, Social and Historical Time. Identity: Personal and Socio-Cultural*, edited by Anita Jacobson-Widding, Atlantic Highlands, Humanities, 1983, pp. 67–91.

MacNally, Richard. *Remembering Trauma*. Cambridge, Mass, Harvard University, Press, 2003.

Marcus, Jacob R. *The Rise and Destiny of the German Jew*. New York: Ktav Publishing, House, 1973.

Markovits, Anderi S. *The German Predicament: Memory and Power in the New Europe*. Ithaca, Cornwell University Press, 1997.

Marshal, Pugh. *Trying to Pin Down Pinter*. Daily Mail, 7 Mar. 1964, pp. 8.

Martin S. Regal. "You Can Only End Once: Ashes to Ashes." *University of Iceland*, vol. 14, 11 Jun. 2008, http://revel.unice.fr/cycnos/index.html?id=1232. Accessed 8 Jan. 2013.

Matthaus & Roseman. *Jewish Response to Persecution: 1933–1938*. Alta Mira, Alta Mira Press, 2010.

Maurice, H. *On Collective Memory*, translated by Lewis A. Coser. Chicago: University of Chicago Press, 1992.

Mead, M. *Continuities in Cultural Evolution*. New Haven, 1964.

Meckien, Richard. *Cultural Memory: The Link between Past, Present and Future*, 3 Jun. 2013, http:www.iea.usp.br/.../

cultural-memory-the-link-between-past-present-and-future. Accessed 18 Feb. 2015.

Merritt, S Hollis. *Pinter in the Play.* Durham & London: Duke University Press, 1990.

Mertz, Johann Baptist. *Faith in History and Society: Towards a Practical Fundamental Theology*. New York, Crossroads, 1980.

Milward, Alan S. *Bad Memories*. The Times Literary Supplement, 14 Apr. 2000, pp. 8.

Miller, Arthur. *Echoes Down the Corridor: Collected Essays 1944–2000*. London, Methuen, 2000.

Misztal, Barbara A. *Theories of Social Remembering*. Philadelphia: Open University Press, 1997. 1 Jul. 2003, http://www.amazon.com. Accessed 17 Mar 2011.

Morgan, O Kenneth. *The People's Peace: British History 1945–1990*. Oxford, Oxford University Press, 1990.

Morrison, Blake. 1 Apr. 2011, http://www.guardian.co.uk/stage/2011/apr/01/harold-pinter-moonlight- blake-morrison. Accessed 7 Jan. 2013.

Munz, Peter. "History and Myth." *Philosophical Quarterly*, vol. 6, 1956, pp. 1–17.

Musil, R. *The Man Without Qualities*. London: Picador, 1979, pp. 436.

Musk, Carol. *Oppressed by Narrative*. New York Times Book Review, Nov. 1994, pp. 18.

Nash, Christopher, editor. *Narrative in Culture: The Uses of Storytelling in the Sciences, Philosophy, and Literature*. New York, Routledge, 1990.

Natar, Wolfgang G. *Literature at War 1914–40: Representing the Time of Greatness in Germany*. New Have, Yale University Press, 1999.

Nayar, Rana. *Intersections: Essays on Indian Literature*. Hyderabad: Orient Black Swan, 2012.

Nelson, Katherine. "Remembering and Telling: a Development Story." *Journal of Narrative and Life History*, vol. 1, no. 2–3, 1994, pp.109–27.

Nietzsche, Friedrich. *The Use and Abuse of History*, translated by Adrian Collins, New York, Macmillan Press, 1957.

Nora, Pierre. "Between Memory and History. Les Lieux de Memoire." *Representations*, no. 26, Spring 1989, pp.7–24.

———. *The Era of Commemoration in Realms of Memory, Symbols*. Paris: Gallimard, 1992.

Novak, Michael. *Story and Experience: Religion as Story*, edited by James Wiggins, New York, Harper and Row, 1975, pp. 175–200.

Novitz, David. "Art, Narrative and Human Nature." *Philosophy and Literature*, vol. 13, no. 1, 1989, pp. 57–74.

Olga, Clendinnen. *Reading the Holocaust*. Cambridge, Cambridge University Press, 1994.

Page, Malcolm, editor. *File on Pinter*. London, Methuen, 1993.

Peacock, D. Keith. *Harold Pinter and the New British Theatre*. London and Westport, Greenwood Press, 1997.

Plunka, Gene. *Holocaust Drama: The Theatre of Atrocity*. Cambridge, New York, Cambridge University Press, 2009.

Prentice, Penelope. *The Pinter Ethic: The Erotic Aesthetic*. New York, Garland, 2000.

Proust, M. *Letters of Marcel Proust*, translated by Mina Curtis, London, Chatto & Windus, 1950.

———. *Remembrance of Things Past*, translated by C.K. Moncrieff and T. Kilmartin, London, 1981.

Reading, Anna. *The Social Inheritance of the Holocaust: Gender, Culture and Memory*. Palgrove, Macmillan Press, 2002. www.amazon.com/social-inheritance-Holocaust-Gender-Culture/dp/0333761472#reader-0333761472. Accessed 15 Mar. 2013.

Remy, Bumppo. *Think Theatre*. 7 Dec. 2011, http://www.remybumppo.org/dramturg-article-pages-334.php. Accessed 5 Mar. 2012.

Renton, Linda. *Pinter and the Object of Desire: An Approach Through Screenplays*. Oxford, Legenda, 2002. (Lacanian kind of analysis).

Ricoeur, Paul. "History as a Narrative and Practice." *Philosophy Today*, vol. 29, 1985, pp. 213–22.

———. "The Human Experience of Time and Narrative." *Research in Phenomenology*, vol. 9, 1979.

Robert, Philip. *The Royal Court Theatre and the Modern Stage*. Cambridge, University Press, 1999.

Rosaldo, Renato. *Culture and Truth*. Boston, Beacon Press, 1989.

Roth, Paul. "How Narrative Explain." *Social Research*, vol. 56, no. 2, Summer 1989, pp. 449–78.

Rodriguez & Fortier. *Cultural Memory: Resistance, Faith and Identity.* USA, University of Texas Press, 2007.

Russel, Robert. "Analysing Narratives in Psychotherapy." *Journal of Narrative and Life History*, vol. 3, no. 4, 1993, pp. 138–55.

Sack, Oliver. *Awakenings*. Picador, 1991.

Sakellaridou, Elizabeth. *Pinter's Female Portraits*. London, Macmillan, 1988.

Sarbin, Theodore. "A Narrative Approach to Repressed Memories." *Journal of Narrative And Life History*, vol. 5, no. 1, 1995, pp. 51–66.

Saunders, Kate. *Pause for Thought*. Sunday Times, 9 Jul. 1995.

Schachter, Daniel L., editor. *Memory Distortion: How Minds, Brains and Societies Reconstruct the Past*. Cambridge, Mass, Harvard University Press, 1995.

———. *The Seven Signs of Memory: How the Mind Forgets and Remembers*. Boston, Houghton Mifflin, 2000.

Schumacher, Claude, editor. *Staging the Holocaust: The Shoah in Drama and Performance*. Cambridge & New York: Cambridge University Press, 2006.

Schuman, Howard, and Jacqueline Scott. "Generations and Collective Memories." *American Sociological Review*, 1989, pp. 359–81.

Schwarcz, Vera. *Bridge Across Broken Time: Chinese and Jewish Cultural Memory*. New Haven & London, Yale University Press, 1998.

Schwartz, Barry. "Iconography and Collective Memory: Lincoln's Image in the American Mind." *Sociological Quarterly*, 1991, pp. 301–19.

———. "Social Context of Commemoration: A Study of Collective Memory." *Social Forces*, 1982), pp. 374–402.

Scolnicov, Hanna. *Pinter's Game of Betrayal*. vol. 14. 11 Jun. 2008, revel.unice.fr/cynos/Index.html?id=1228 11 June 2008. Accessed 7 Nov. 2012.

Scott, Michael, editor. *Harold Pinter: The Birthday Party, The Caretaker, The Homecoming*. London: Macmillan Press, 1993.

Silverst Sturken, Marita. *Narratives of Recovery: Repressed Memory as Cultural Memory*, edited by Mieke Bal, Jonathan V. Crewe and Leo Spitzer, *Acts Of Memory: Cultural Recall in the Present*, Hanover, Dartmouth College Press, 1999.

Strunk, Volker, editor. *Harold Pinter: Towards a Politics of His Plays*. New York, 1989.

Silverstein, Marc. *Harold Pinter and the Language of Cultural Power.* London and Toronto, Associated University Press, 1993.

Southard, E.E. *Shell-Shock and Other Neuropsychiatric Problems Presented in Five Hundred and Eighty-Nine Case Histories From the War Literature: 1914–18*. Boston, W.M. Leonard, 1919.

Stone, Lawrence. *The Past and the Present*. Boston, Routledge and Kegan Paul, 19891

Summers, Ian. *Breaking the Silence*. London, London Daily News, 19 Jun. 1987, pp. 19.

———. *A Conscientious Objector*. Independent, 18 Oct. 1988, pp. 9–17.

Susan, Williams. *Cultural Memory: How We See Ourselves as a People and Nation*. Bloomington, Indiana University Press, 25 Apr. 2003, pp. 2–3.

Syke, B. Lloyd. *No Man's Land: Review*. blogscrikey.com.au/curtain call/2011/11/7/ Review-no-man's-land-drama-theatre-Sydney 7 November 2011. Accessed 7 Nov. 2012.

Taylor, J. Russell. *Anger and After*. London, Methuen, 1962.

Terdiman, R. *Present Past Modernity and the Memory Crisis*. http// www.amazon.com: Present Past; Modernity and the Memory Crisis (9780801481321). Accessed 22 Jun. 2011.

Thompson, David T. *Pinter: The Players' Playwright*. London & New York, Macmillan, 1985.

Todman, Dan. *The Great War: Myth and Memory*. London, Hambledon and London, 2005.

Trussller, Simon. *The Plays of Harold Pinter*. London, Victor Gollancz, 1973.

Turner, Victor. *From Ritual to Theatre: The Human Seriousness of Play*. New York, Performing Arts Journal Publications, 1982.

Vansina, Jan. *Oral Tradition as History*. Madison, University of Wisconsin Press, 1985.

Walsh, John. *That Nice Mr. Pinter*. Independent, 8 Feb. 1999, pp. 8.

Watson, David. *Against Forgetting. Utne Reader*. Mar./Apr. 1994, pp. 112–15.

Weintraub, Stanley. "Autobiography and Historical Consciousness." *Critical Inquiry*, vol. 1, no. 4, 1975, pp. 171–93.

White, Hayden. *The Content of Form: Narrative Discourse and Historical Representation*. Baltimore, Johns Hopkins University Press, 1987.

Williams, Susan. "Cultural Memory: How We See as a People and Nation." *Bloomington: Indiana University Press*, 25 Apr. 2003, http://www.homepages.indiana.edu/042503/text/memorywar.html. Accessed .

Winter, J. *Remembering War: The Great War Between Memory and History*. New Haven and London, Yale University Press, 2006.

Winter, J., and Emmanuel S., editors. "*Framework" in War and Remembrance in the 20th Century*. Cambridge, Cambridge University Press,, 1999, pp. 1–39.

Winter, Jay, and Emmanuel, S., editors. *War and Remembrance: In the 20th Century.* Cambridge, Cambridge University Press, Oct. 2009, http://www.amazon.com. Accessed 15 Mar. 2011.

Worth, Katherine. *Joyce via Pinter: Revolutions in Modern English Drama*. London, G. Bells 7 Sons, 1973.

Young, James E., Ed. *The Art of Memory: Holocaust Memorials in History*. Munich, Prestel, 1994.

———. *The Texture of Memory: Holocaust Memorials and Meaning*. New Haven, Yale University Press, 1993.

Zerubavel, Eviatar. *Time Maps: Collective Memory.* Chicago: University Press, 2003. 1 Nov. 2004. http://www.amazon.com. Accessed.

Zerubavel, Yael. *Recovered Roots: Collective Memory and the Making of Israeli National Tradition*. Chicago, University of Chicago Press, 1995.

Index